0524

€2 49
N
40

48-009-01

Due Back
8.12.97   15-12-97

THE LITTLE BLACK BOOK OF BUSINESS LETTERS

Michael C. Thomsett

amacom
American Management Association

This book is available at a special
discount when ordered in bulk quantities.
For information, contact Special Sales Department,
AMACOM, a division of American Management Association,
135 West 50th Street, New York, NY 10020.

LIBRARY OF CONGRESS
Library of Congress Cataloging-in-Publication Data

Thomsett, Michael C.
  The little black book of business letters / Michael C. Thomsett.
    p.   cm.
  Includes index.
ISBN 0-8144-7694-5
  1. Commercial correspondence. 2. Letter-writing. I. Title.
HF5721.T46   1988   88-14736
651.7'5—dc19   CIP

Printing number

10 9 8 7 6 5 4

For
my
son,
Michael Paul

Contents

Introduction

"Writing comes more easily if you have something to say."

—Sholem Asch

There are two secrets to writing good, effective business letters: You must understand your reader, and you must know what you're trying to say. Good letters are simple. They get to the point, provide needed information, and conclude with action points or ideas: Simple phrasing is used, and long words or technical jargon are avoided as much as possible.

A letter does more than convey information or request a response. It also tells a lot about you. It conveys your personality by the choice of words, neatness, spelling, and tone of expression. A letter going outside your company also tells a lot about the organization. If written communications are the first form of contact with others, they can make or break a future business relationship.

Many business letters lack the clarity of communication necessary to get results. This book explains how to construct business letters to maximize their effect. It discusses the proper formatting of business letters and provides useful tips for improving writing skills. Each chapter concludes with work projects, so that you can test your skills as you read. Answers and further suggestions are included in the first appendix, and reference material on punctuation and usage is in the second appendix. With this book, you will learn how to write letters that get action,

1

bring out a response in others, and improve your ability to achieve results.

Keep your little black book in your desk at all times, and refer to it often. Don't leave it in plain sight, as other employees may be inclined to borrow it. If this book is lost, you can trace it by reading the letters other people are writing. Look for a noticeable improvement in style, pride in the use of language, and a new ability to make others act. Then you will know where your little black book may be found.

1

Why You Write Letters: Defining Your Purpose

"He can compress the most words into the smallest idea of any man I ever met."

—Abraham Lincoln

"I got your letter today," Marilyn told Ted over the phone. "To tell you the truth, I'm confused. I want to respond, but I'm not sure what you're asking for." Ted could not recall the letter, so Marilyn began reading it to him. He interrupted after two sentences, and apologized. "Oh, that was just a practice letter. We wanted to see how well our new typewriter worked."

All of us have received letters that never get to the main point, or to any point at all. But you write a letter to convey a message and create a response, so you should always clearly state why you are writing and what you expect. As fundamental as this requirement seems, a large number of letters lack clear statements.

A simple letter depends on clarity of thought. Before you even start to write, make sure you have a clear idea of what you want to achieve—your purpose—and then organize your thoughts around that.

3

WHAT IS YOUR PURPOSE?

There are four reasons to write a letter:

1. *To convey or request information*. Several common types fall into this category: letters that convey or request an answer, respond to a proposal sent in by an outside supplier, or advise a job applicant of a decision, for example.

2. *To persuade*. A sales letter, for example, attempts to convince someone else to buy your product or services. A letter to subordinates, assigning work, should persuade them to respond.

3. *To complain*. You may need to write a supplier, expressing dissatisfaction with a product. Or you may have the responsibility of answering a complaint from someone.

4. *To compliment*. Any letter can have a complimentary tone, but some are written specifically to thank someone or to acknowledge an exceptionally good job. Recognition is important to everyone, and the unexpected complimentary letter creates tremendous goodwill, whether the recipient is an outside provider or an employee.

Getting Organized

Organize your thoughts with four preparation steps (see Figure 1-1). Make sure you understand them *before* you begin to write.

The first step is to define your message. Once you know that, the hardest part of the letter is already written. Before drafting your letter, write down—on a separate piece of paper—the main message you want to communicate. In a complaint letter, the main message is "We are very upset that you didn't come through." The message of a complimentary letter is "You did a good job and we appreciate it." Too many letters go back and forth between two or more separate ideas; this lack of organization creates confusion. Everything in your letter should be directly related to the primary message.

The next step is to list the major points you want to communicate, then arrange them in order of importance. You will discuss them in that order in your final letter.

Figure 1-1. Preparing your letter.

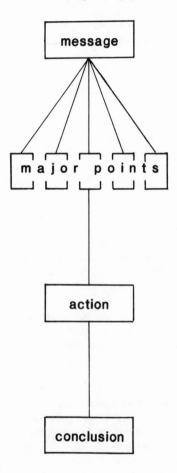

The third step is to write down the desired action—either what you want the reader to do in response to your letter, or what you intend to do.

In the last step, plan your conclusion: What do you intend to ask? You can end with an action point, a compliment, a deadline, or some other appropriate statement. But make it forceful: a letter that trails off weakly is not likely to stay in the reader's mind.

If you have these four preparation phases in mind when you begin to compose a letter, the job will be much easier.

The Information Letter

Use the four-step preparation technique to organize your thoughts. For example, here's the first draft of a letter asking for information. Do you think the writer mentally prepared first? How would you improve the letter?

Dear _____:

We are compiling a report on the feasibility of redesigning our work space to improve efficiency and access from one work station to another.

The modular open space concept you demonstrated at the recent design convention was most interesting to us. We would like to know how much time would be required to evaluate and redesign our offices.

We have experienced difficulty in making the best use of space, with several enclosed offices and a large central floor space. We are convinced that with better design, we could facilitate a planned expansion, fit more work area into the floor plan, and create the feeling of openness and more space.

Please supply us with a range of costs, including alternatives in materials you use on panels. We are also interested in the relative quality versus cost, and will want to know about sound insulation in an open office area.

Please have your local representative contact us as soon as possible.

Sincerely,

If the primary message is identified first, the request can be stated much more clearly. The message is "We are interested in the service you provide, and want to hear more." Major points include concern with cost, material quality, insulation, and the time required to evaluate and redesign the office. The action point is to ask for the local representative to call.

Here's a reorganized version of the letter:

[Edited]

Dear _____:

We were very impressed with the modular open space concept you demonstrated at the recent office design convention, and would like to know more.

Please have your local representative contact us for an appointment as soon as possible. We ask that at our first meeting, the following questions be addressed:

1. How much will be required to evaluate our redesign needs?
2. How many hours must we expect to lose in productive time because of redesign work?
3. What design and material choices do you offer?
4. What do those alternatives cost?
5. What degree of sound insulation should we expect?

We look forward to hearing from you in the very near future, and hope that you can help us solve our space problems.

Sincerely,

In this more organized form, the letter clearly states what you want and raises the issues you expect the representative to be prepared to answer.

A request for information can be less formal when it is written to another person in your own organization. In many of the samples in this chapter, we refer to communications between managers within a company as letters. In actual practice, internal messages usually take the form of memos rather than letters. The distinction is one of format rather than content. Memos do not have address, salutation, and signature blocks. Keep in mind that some examples may take memo form in your organization, depending on your company's policies and practices. You can also assume that certain facts are generally known and that detailed explanations backing up your request are not necessary. Your emphasis should be on direct explanation, simplicity, and a less-than-formal tone.

Example: You need to write to a division vice president, requesting additional information. The first draft reads:

Dear _____:

We are in receipt of your monthly production status report for October. However, in order to complete our own analysis, we need additional information.

Please provide complete details on orders placed but not yet submitted for fulfillment, broken down by both product type and sales representative. Our monthly estimate must be based not only upon orders completed but also upon an estimate of pending orders. This is necessary so that we may place orders, control inventory, and plan for cash flow and working capital controls in the immediate future. All of this is contingent upon receiving full and complete information from every division.

We anticipate a quick response from you, as our task cannot be completed until you comply with this request.

Sincerely,

Several points about this letter are flawed. First, the middle paragraph is unnecessarily wordy; it should be edited down to two short sentences. Second, the letter's tone is unfriendly and demanding; you are more likely to get a willing response if you use a more personal tone. Third, while the letter asks for additional information, it does not indicate the format to be used, so chances are, this will not be the last time you will have to make your request. Most significant, the letter does not specify a deadline; it only asks for a "quick response."

An internal letter such as this should not have to explain generally known facts. You can assume, for example, that a vice president already knows you need to include full information in your reports. Here is a redrafted form of this letter that is clearer and better focused:

[Edited]

Dear _____:

    Thank you for the October production summary, which arrived today.

    We have expanded our monthly status report to include all pending orders, in addition to orders already placed. Please send in a breakdown, as of October 31, of all orders in pending status, using the same format as before.

    We'd appreciate receiving this information before November 15. If that's a problem, please call me and we can get the details over the phone. I'll look forward to hearing from you soon.

                 Sincerely,

When you write a letter to communicate information, you will be less concerned with tone. When you make a request, you must be aware of how the reader will interpret your letter, But when *you* are asked for something, the straightforward response is always preferable.

You still want to avoid generally known facts. And if the request is for a large volume of information, your response should take the form of a report. In cases where it will take time to prepare your response, write a letter explaining the delay and promise to deliver your report within a reasonable time. And make sure that your response does answer the question or supply the information requested.

Example: A customer writes to the manager in a company's shipping department and asks how long it would take to complete deliveries in the future. The request reads: "We occasionally have rush orders and will ask you for a fast response. Can you promise to fill orders within one week?"

The manager's first draft reads:

Dear _____:

Thank you for your letter of January 11. We always attempt to complete orders in the most expedient way possible. Last year, we filled 78 percent of all orders within three weeks or less.

We often encounter problems beyond our control, because of backorders with our own suppliers, delays in deliveries, or overloads in our traffic department. In heavy volume periods, fulfillment tends to take longer than we like. We anticipate these problems whenever possible and attempt to schedule deliveries for the greatest convenience of our customers.

Your orders should be filled within three weeks in the majority of cases. And while we cannot promise a one-week delivery, we will make every attempt to respond as quickly as possible.

Sincerely,

The problem is that the letter does not answer the question. Obviously, the shipping department cannot guarantee one-week responses in all cases. But to respond by saying that 78 percent of all orders are sent within *three* weeks is not the point. The letter should focus on the question. A revised draft:

[Edited]

Dear _____:

In response to your inquiry of January 11, we can promise to give you every consideration and will often be able to complete one-week deliveries. But we cannot guarantee one-week fulfillment in every case.

I suggest that when you need priority treatment the chances of a fast delivery will be improved if you take these steps:

1. Hand-deliver or send by express mail all orders requiring fast response.
2. Write the date you would like delivery on your order. If that date is within three weeks, highlight it.
3. Call me and place the order by phone. We will still need the written requisition, but if I know about the order in advance, I can place it on the schedule and assign it priority.
4. If you can anticipate a rush order in the near future, let me know as quickly as possible.

When we are aware of a rush job, we will make every effort to fill your orders quickly. In most cases, a one-week schedule will be possible. But at times scheduling, backorder, and traffic delays make one-week fulfillment impossible.

Please let me know if I can provide you with any other information concerning our fulfillment procedures. I will look forward to speaking with you soon.

Sincerely,

In this version, the question is addressed directly and suggestions are given that would improve the likelihood of a fast response. The manager also warns that he cannot promise a one-week delivery in every case. This is the best possible answer.

The Persuasion Letter

While the information letter conveys or asks for facts, a persuasion letter requires more selling. You have to accept the notion that your memos and letters may not be read or understood; if you're writing persuasively, you need to be even more careful.

Have you ever written a letter that needed a follow-up communication some weeks later? Chances are, you neglected to include certain specific elements to create the answer you wanted. For example, you must ask for a specific action or series of actions and provide your reader with a deadline. You may have to explain why you need the information, and you may also have to tell the recipient how to do the work you need.

Example: You write to another manager, requesting the temporary assignment of one employee to help you compile a report. Your first draft reads:

Dear _____:

    I have been given the assignment of analyzing employee efficiency and workload in both of our departments, so that needed adjustments in personnel can be made.

    This analysis will be based on a detailed study of overtime, employee workload trends, and skill levels. We will study trends over the last six months. Since the study also involves your department, I will need your participation.

    I suggest that you assign one of your employees to work with me. We will coordinate the gathering and organization of data so that the report will be consistent and complete. I estimate this temporary assignment will require three days of work.

    This report's deadline is imminent. I would like to work on it early next week. Please let me know at once who you will assign to work with me.

Sincerely,

This version lacks the elements that will persuade another manager to cooperate. Its dictatorial and unfriendly tone is likely to create a defensive or angry answer rather than willing cooperation.

A better version reads:

[*Revised*]

Dear _____:

The executive committee has asked me to compile a summary of employee efficiency and workload in both of our departments.

The report is likely to lead to adjustments in personnel, which will affect both of us. I encourage you to work with me on this project, so that the report will be fair and impartial.

I suggest that we meet next week, at your convenience, to develop a format and identify the most practical way to proceed. When we meet, I will also ask you to assign someone in your department to work with me in gathering information. If you have any other ideas about how to proceed, I will welcome your participation. And of course, I intend to put both of our names on the final report.

I've been given a deadline of February 10, so I'd like to get started as soon as possible. Can we meet next Monday to discuss the best way to proceed?

Sincerely,

This second version clearly states what you need and want, explains the project, and includes the other manager as a participant. By taking this approach, you are more likely to get a cooperative response. At the same time, you avoid offending or threatening your colleague. If the other manager would prefer an alternative to what you suggest, this letter leaves the question open.

Whenever you ask for something from another department, you must be aware of the territorial factor. If you impose too much, demand an immediate response, or assume that the other person will drop everything to help you, you'll get poor results. A friendly letter, asking directly for help but without making assumptions, will create a favorable response.

The Complaint Letter

The human touch improves your letters, whether the message is positive or negative. Complaint letters require a special form of directness and tact. You certainly want to leave no doubt about what you are saying, but you must still be aware of how someone else will receive your words. A poorly written complaint letter may create exactly the opposite response from the one you want. If the tone is offensive, the recipient may refuse to correct a problem.

Include several elements in your complaint letter:

- Address it to an individual who will have the position and authority to take action, correct shortcomings in procedures, and ensure that problems will not be repeated.
- Identify yourself by title and responsibility. Doing so will help put your letter in perspective. For example, if the reader is a supplier and you explain that you have the primary responsibility for choosing suppliers, your complaint will have greater impact than if your role is unstated.
- Explain the situation in a briefly stated but complete sequence of events. Leave out any emotional expressions in this section, no matter how tempted you are to emote in writing. (A suggestion: Write a first draft in which you let out all of your anger. Get it out of your system and then edit the emotion out of the final draft.)
- Always state specifically what you expect as a response and how you would like the problem to be resolved.

Example: A manager in a manufacturing company writes a complaint letter to a supplier. The first draft reads:

Dear _____:

We communicated with you on July 10 regarding our need for the immediate delivery of several hundred pounds of stainless steel. As has been the case often in the past, our need was immediate and urgent, as we were up against a production deadline. We depended on your immediate response, but did not receive it.

Your employee was less than cooperative on the telephone, but did reluctantly promise to deliver the order the same day. We made repeated requests during the day for the delivery, and finally contacted another supplier. The order was then delivered without problem. Your order did not arrive until three days later, in spite of our appeals for immediate delivery. By the time it did show up, we no longer needed it, and it was returned.

This problem may lead us to seek another supplier in the future.

Sincerely,

That's a strong letter, but it does not get to the point quickly enough. It also closes with the weak statement "may lead us to seek. . . ." A better way to make the point is to state the case as quickly as possible in the opening, and specify what is expected in the way of response:

[Edited]

Dear _____:

We are deeply concerned with a situation that has developed because of your delivery procedures.

As manager of our purchasing department, I am responsbile for ensuring that our own production schedule is maintained. Accordingly, I select dependable suppliers whose promises can be relied upon. Last week, the following events occurred:

1. We placed an order on July 10 for several hundred pounds of stainless steel, and were promised delivery on the same day.
2. When the order did not arrive by 1 p.m., I called your

warehouse and was told the shipment would be here within one hour.

3. I called again at 2 p.m. Your employee, who identified himself only as Frank, would not state when the order was shipped or even if it had left your warehouse. He hung up on me when I asked for more specifics.

4. I called back at once, and Frank refused to give me any information about the status of the order. He also refused to give me the name of his supervisor.

5. The order did not arrive that day, and we finally placed another with one of your competitors. It was filled immediately.

6. Three days later, your order came. We refused delivery.

I bring this problem to your attention and hope that it was an isolated incident. Can you promise that similar situations will not occur in the future? We would like to continue our long-standing relationship with you, but only on condition that our reasonable requests will be met and that promises will be kept. Otherwise, we will place future orders elsewhere.

Sincerely,

This second letter states the case much more strongly. It also gives the reader a clear choice: Either correct the problem or lose our business.

Sometimes your task is not to write a complaint letter but to answer one. When you receive a complaint letter, you should respond by stating exactly how you plan to correct a problem. But be sure you can actually do it. Promising something you can't deliver is worse than not responding at all. For example, you receive a letter complaining that a customer representative was rude during a service call. Your answer includes the statement:

I will meet with the manager of the service department and make sure that disciplinary action is taken.

Will you actually meet with the manager? Do you have the authority to carry through your claim? And more to the point: Is this a solution?

One alternative is to promise in your letter to bring the problem to the manager's attention and then personally ask that manager to get in touch with the customer directly. You can also thank the reader for informing you of the problem and promise to review service procedures so that the problem will not recur.

An appropriate response to a complaint could read:

Dear _____:

Thank you for bringing to my attention the problem you encountered with our customer service department.

I have ordered an immediate review of that department's procedures, so that incidents like this will not be repeated in the future. The service manager has assured me that the incident is under review and that appropriate and immediate action will be taken.

Our policy has always been to provide our customers with the highest quality of service, and we certainly attempt to anticipate problems before they occur. Unfortunately, no procedure can possibly correct or safeguard against every shortcoming. But we do appreciate having heard from you, and we promise to respond quickly. To that end, I have asked the service manager to contact you directly to ensure that your original service request is resolved at once.

If for any reason you are not entirely satisfied with our response, please contact me directly.

Sincerely,

The Complimentary Letter

Always be specific and direct in your letters, and stay with your primary focus. Writing a letter that thanks someone and acknowledges exceptional performance creates valuable goodwill. This type of letter is especially noteworthy because it's voluntary; the reader notices and remembers your effort to show your appreciation.

However, when you write a complimentary letter, make sure your tone matches your message. Here's the first draft of a letter thanking a supplier for a good job:

Dear _____:

It has come to my attention that you recently assisted us with a rush order. We needed several reams of paper on the day we called, and your employees were able to fill the order.

We know that normal procedures call for a seven-day lapse between order and delivery, and we appreciate your responsive-ness in exception to this requirement.

Thank you for this consideration. We will place many future orders with you.

Sincerely,

You can improve this rather cold and uninteresting letter with a little editing:

[Edited]

Dear _____:

Thank you so much for your fast response last week. It's refresh-ing to experience good customer service and friendly, motivated employees.

We needed several reams of paper immediately, and the order was filled without delay. I know you usually require a full week to fill an order, and we appreciate your making an exception for us.

You can count on us for many future orders. We're all looking forward to a long and satisfying relationship.

Sincerely,

Internal letters or memos that acknowledge good work help maintain high morale in your department. A common complaint among employees is that their managers notice them only when there's a problem, and that good work is rarely or never acknowledged. Everyone appreciates recognition.

It takes so little effort to write a brief memo:

Dear Tom:

Thanks for coming through on the status report, especially on such short notice.

It was thorough and accurate, and I appreciate your extra effort. It's good to know I can depend on you under pressure.

Sincerely,

Anyone can write an excellent business letter. The secret is not in possessing talent or special skill but in being willing to take the time to identify your reasons for writing and then organizing your letter around them. Clear thinking leads to clear writing. And that's not so much a natural talent as a work habit you can develop with practice.

WORK PROJECT

1. Rewrite the following requests to soften their tone:

   a. We must have your response by Friday.
   b. You must comply with these requirements at once.
   c. Do not miss the deadline, as you did last month.

2. How would you rewrite these opening statements?

   a. Recognizing the importance of the pending deadline for the monthly report, I must insist on a quick response.

   b. I urgently suggest that we meet at once to resolve the problem we
      both face.
   c. We appreciate the effort you put forth to comply with our recent
      request.

3. Rewrite these three closing statements:

   a. Your deadline is next Wednesday.
   b. Please advise if extra help is needed.
   c. We would like to believe that this oversight will not be repeated.

2

Write to Create Response: Prompting Others to Action

"Our admiration of fine writing will always be in proportion to its real difficulty and its apparent ease."

—Charles Caleb Colton

"I don't understand why Bob hasn't answered my memos," Frank told his manager. "I've made a point of staying in touch, and I added a few personal comments whenever I wrote. But my last three requests went unanswered."

The manager smiled and shook his head. "I guess you didn't hear. Bob retired two months ago."

You get the response you expect only if you deserve to. That means your letters must be planned carefully and written in the tone that is right for the circumstances.

As a writer of effective business letters, you are faced with two problems: creating a desired response to the letters you write, and

21

deciding how to respond to someone else's letter. This chapter deals with both problems.

KEEP THE READER IN MIND

Use Appropriate Tone

There are two versions of every message: what you mean to convey, and what is received. Even the most carefully stated message can be misunderstood, and the carelessly phrased request can create angry refusal instead of cheerful compliance.

Empathy with your reader makes your letters easier to write and improves their chances for a good reception. But in the real world, chances are you know little or nothing about the reader's personality. So how can you critically review your own letters from the reader's point of view?

There's no need for ESP. You can cultivate the skill for writing a perceptive letter by making a series of reasonable assumptions. If you are writing to a fellow manager, you must certainly know how a manager perceives messages. How would you react to the same communication? When you write a memo or letter to an employee, think back to how you felt when you held a similar position. When you correspond with an executive, supplier, or customer, use your reasoning and common sense to understand your message from the other person's perspective.

Failing to grasp another person's point of view is a common pitfall in business. There is a natural tendency for all of us to assume that our own perspectives are the only valid ones. If you are in a position of constantly asking for help from others, you might tend to see your own work as being more important than anything else that goes on in the company and to place a lower priority on what others do. That's a pitfall. But you can get around that problem and, in the process, improve understanding and cooperation within your company. It never hurts to demonstrate in your letters that you understand the reader's perceptions. In fact, demonstrating that you do comprehend will only add to your success.

Example: An accounting manager wrote this letter to the director of marketing:

Dear _____:

    We're going through our monthly budget review, and find that your department has again exceeded its travel and entertainment budget.

    Please send me a complete explanation of this variance as soon as possible. I need to complete my report by the 15th, so I'd appreciate a prompt response.

    Can I get your report by the end of the week?

Sincerely,

The director of marketing called the accounting manager by phone and angrily protested. "You accountants have no idea what it's like meeting with customers and staying on our production schedule. You just sit in your offices preparing reports." The accounting manager, who was hardly expecting an angry response, realized too late that the *tone* of his letter was wrong for this situation. Of course, marketing and accounting people are like the farmers and the ranchers of the corporate world: One doesn't understand why the other builds fences. An extra effort must be made to break those fences down.

In this case, the accounting manager had no chance to formulate a response, because by the time he'd taken a breath, the marketing director had already hung up. So he drafted another letter:

Dear _____:

    I must apologize for creating a misunderstanding between us. The tone of my last letter was offensive to you, I now realize, and that was not my intention.

    On the contrary, I depend upon you to provide information in order to perform my job, and I do respect the work you do. During the last year, for example, you increased sales volume by more than 45 percent, and profits by 21 percent. That's an admirable record. Perhaps our failure is in not communicating more frequently, and in limiting our correspondence to requests when problems arise.

Part of my job is compiling a monthly report that explains to management why budgets are being exceeded. I suspect that in this case, the original budget was not adequate, based on sales volume. The variance in travel and entertainment is probably justified by the related favorable variance in our income forecast.

I would like to meet with you at your convenience during the coming week, and would appreciate the opportunity to discuss the variance with you. Can we get together on Wednesday?

Sincerely,

If the accounting manager had thought ahead and anticipated how his message might be interpreted, he would have used a far different tone for his request and would never have to agonize over the letter of apology. In the revised version, the entire tone is positive and the request is not the initial focus:

[Revised]

Dear _____:

Congratulations on the impressive sales volume you and your department have generated this year. A favorable variance in the income account is exactly the kind of problem we accountants like to be faced with.

Because the volume is so much higher than anyone expected, variable expenses have also been higher. That has created an unfavorable variance in some accounts, notably in travel and entertainment. I'm confident that this small problem is easily explained as a direct consequence of higher sales, and that we will conclude a budget revision is in order.

To make that determination, I would like to meet with you next

week. If you can spare 30 minutes to help me go over the figures,
I will appreciate your help.
   I'm looking forward to seeing you, so that we can develop an
explanation that will satisfy management. Can we get together
on Wednesday?

Sincerely,

In this case, the request concerns a problem, but the letter is positive
throughout. Rather than focusing on that negative, the request is made
in the context of the larger, positive trend. Taking this more diplomatic
approach makes allies of the two departments and defuses any possible
hard feelings.

A difference in point of view also arises between employees at different
levels in the organization. It is especially difficult for a supervisor to ask
for something from a top executive. Here's how a request can be given
to an executive without creating a negative response:

Dear _____:

   This department has been given the job of compiling the
annual report for the year just ended. I understand that you have
written the financial section of this report in the past.
   Our deadline for final copy is February 16, so I would like to
compile all sections for final review by January 31.
   If this fits with your own schedule, I'd like to meet with you
next week. Otherwise, we will need to alter our typesetting
and printing schedule. When will it be convenient to meet?

Sincerely,

Be sensitive to the way someone else will read your letter. Careless use
of words can often pervert your intention, creating confusion about your

request and your attitude. Read your drafts from the recipient's point of view, looking for phrases that might create a misunderstanding. Then edit yourself to remove those problems.

Editing is especially important when closing your letter so that you end with a strong point. Here's a technique that will help you create stronger letters: List your requests on a separate sheet of paper, and next to them write out the recipient's probable responses (see Figure 2–1). Then be sure to address those points in your letter.

Ask for Response

You can expect a response only if you indicate what it should be. If you're asking for a report, request the format and a deadline. If your

Figure 2-1. Planning the response.

request   possible
                                     response

1.

2.

3.

letter requires an answer, ask for it. And if any other action must be taken by the recipient, be as clear as possible about what you expect.

Compare two endings to a letter asking for a report:

[*Weak Ending*]

When you have completed this report, please submit it to me.

[*Strong Ending*]

We need this information no later than the 10th. Please contact me at once if there's any problem in meeting this deadline. Otherwise, I will look forward to seeing the report.

If you do not receive a response or are not sure that one is in the works, follow up with another letter asking for the status of the project or report. Be especially cautious to phrase your status request so that the reader is not offended.

Example: One manager writes to another as follows:

Dear _____:

I wrote to you a week ago about the information I need for my report. To date, I have not received a reply.

Please let me know immediately whether or not you will be able to provide me with the information.

Sincerely,

This note will be interpreted as aggressive, even if your attitude when writing it was friendly. It could be revised, though:

[Revised]

Dear _____:

Following up on my request of last week, I am awaiting your response in order to complete my report.

Please get in touch as soon as possible and let me know when I can expect this information. Thank you for your help.

Sincerely,

Revising a letter to correct its tone is neither difficult nor time-consuming. Invest a few minutes to organize your letter, identify the primary message, and allow for possible reactions, and your written communications will be much more effective.

Letters That Get Responses

The challenge is to get what you need without offending the other person. Communicating both to the outside and within an organization should be thought of as operating a panel of buttons. You need to push the right ones to make a green light go on. If you push the wrong ones, nothing happens—or maybe you get an electric shock!

You certainly want that green light as often as possible. This requires developing a sensitivity that allows you to see your letters from the other person's perspective. How will your deadlines and requests be received? Once you know that, you can build your letters to increase the green lights and reduce the blanks or the electric shocks.

Example: You write a letter to the manager of the production department, requesting her participation in an interdepartmental presentation. Your first draft reads:

Dear _____:

The president of our newly acquired subsidiary, Research Consulting Corp., is scheduled to visit our offices on August 11–13.

We are preparing a series of short presentations by each department, running 5 to 10 minutes each. Your deadline for submitting a first draft of your presentation is one week from today.

Upon review, you will then be expected to present a final version by August 1.

Sincerely,

You can expect a negative reaction to this letter. Its tone is demanding and unfriendly. The deadline is not requested, it's imposed. Even if you do not intend to convey such a message, this letter will certainly be read that way. A different version of the same request could read:

[Revised]

Dear _____:

We are organizing a series of short departmental presentations to welcome the president of our newly acquired subsidiary, Research Consulting Corp.

He is scheduled to visit our offices from August 11 to 13. Each department manager is encouraged to prepare a 5 minute presentation.

Please submit your first draft one week from today and plan a final draft by August 1.

We look forward to seeing your first draft and to your help in orienting our new division's president.

Sincerely,

This version describes the presentations as a joint effort. That form of communication is more likely to bring about cooperation.

Cooperation between departments is preferable to the isolated territorial attitude that too often finds its way into letters. When you write in a demanding tone, you only build the walls higher. Strive to make the recipient of your letters feel equal to you; it builds trust. Ask—don't demand—and you will get what you need.

If you have had difficulty with business letters in the past, you can improve your track record by adding another step: Communicate in person or on the telephone. Precede a letter with a call; you can explain exactly what you need, eliminate any misperceptions, and then follow up with a brief letter. Another way is to follow a letter with a call; you'll get the same improvement in communication. The same followup technique applies to letters written to people outside your company. They can be just as territorial as department heads on the inside. So be aware of tone when asking for help.

Example: A manager working on a budget writes to a supplier to determine future pricing policies. The first draft reads:

Dear _____:

I am working on my departmental budget for the new year. In analyzing last year's supply expenses, I notice that you raised prices by 5 percent in June. Do you know of any planned price increases in the coming year?

Our management has instructed us to thoroughly analyze our expenses for this budget and to seek ways to reduce expenses wherever possible. So your cooperation will be appreciated.

I need a response no later than one week from this Friday. Thank you for your help.

Sincerely,

This letter includes an implied threat, which is probably unintentional. After mentioning last year's price increase, it states that management wants to reduce expenses. The letter could be seen as a request for a commitment to not raise prices. It implies that if prices are raised the supplier will lose the company's business.

That's not what the request is all about. To get a fast, cooperative response, this letter should be simplified and better expressed. For example:

Dear _____:

I am preparing a departmental budget for the new year. Our management has required us to thoroughly support any expense increases with solid information, rather than depending on estimates.

Do you anticipate any scheduled price increases during the coming year? If so, I would like to adjust my estimates of supply expenses as part of the budget.

I've been given a tight deadline for completing my budget. If you can respond before next Friday, I'll appreciate your help.

Sincerely,

In this version, there's no implied threat of taking business elsewhere. The request is explained clearly and the deadline is specific. The supplier should gladly respond with the information requested.

Three Possible Responses

Communication is a complicated matter. More can go wrong than right in the process, just because people will not always understand your written word in the same way you intend it. Each written communication contains a chain of actions and possible reactions.

Your original letter requests action or some other form of response. The person who receives your letter can react in one of three ways (see also Figure 2-2):

Figure 2-2. Responses to letters.

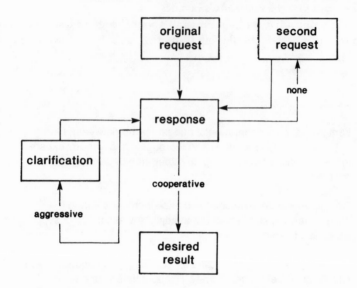

1. *By failing to respond at all.* If someone fails to even answer your letter, it probably means you didn't make your request specific enough. Always give the reader a clear idea of what you need, and ask for a response. Don't assume that someone will interpret what you need and then supply it.

The "no response" response leads to a second request. You have to ask again, either in person or with another letter, which delays the final response and wastes your time. Avoid both by making your first communication clear. If you receive no response, you can send a second letter. But if the problem is that your first letter was not read, the chances are your second one won't be either. Consider the direct approach and use one of these techniques:

- Visit the other person and discuss what you need face-to-face. Follow up your meeting with a memo or letter that states what you requested and what was promised.

- Telephone the other person and ask for a response. Follow up with a memo confirming the discussion.
- If you cannot get an acceptable response, take the matter to your supervisor.

2. *Aggressively*. If your letter is interpreted as offensive or too demanding, you can expect a poor reaction. If, for example, you ask for information in such a way that someone thinks you are telling him what to do, or that you're not going through the chain of command properly, or that you're asking him to do your work for you, you are bound to get an aggressive response.

To avoid the delay and poor relationships that this misunderstanding creates, carefully phrase your requests so that they won't be perceived as power plays. This is especially important in communications with others in your own organization. If you send a message that creates an aggressive response, it will impede communications—and not just for the immediate request, but in the future, too.

Mistrust and antagonism between departments is a difficult problem that is resolved only with demonstrated goodwill and hard work. A gap is easily created when a carelessly worded letter goes out. It may require many months of your energy to undo the problem.

You can prevent aggressive responses and the consequent ill will by being perfectly clear in every letter and memo you send out. If mistrust develops, don't depend on a well-written letter to undo the damage. Confront problems by meeting with the other person and working out your differences.

3. *Cooperatively*. This is, of course, the most desirable form of response. You ask for something and it is given to you—without delay and without friction. Unfortunately, this is also the rarest form of response. Too often, your best intentions are lost when the written word is used. We communicate much better in person, when any misperceptions can be raised and explained on the spot.

You improve the odds of a cooperative response by following up your letter with a personal meeting. This is especially appropriate when you need a response by a deadline, when the issue is sensitive in nature, or when the issue is complex.

Include in your letter a request for a meeting or set up a meeting and bring your letter with you when you go. Then the issues can be discussed in person. If any problems or misunderstandings develop, you can resolve them immediately.

YOUR OWN RESPONSE LETTER

An equal amount of diplomacy is required in your responses to others. When you receive a letter asking for information, say, or assigning a task to you, the way you respond will either improve internal relationships or make them worse. Just as someone else can offend you, you might offend in turn by the tone of your response.

Example: A new manager is overwhelmed by the massive assignments from the president of the company. During his first week, he has received two letters assigning major projects, each with immediate deadlines. Another manager tells him that the president is in the habit of writing rambling assignment letters, most of which never go beyond the request phase. But the new manager feels he should respond in some way. One letter has instructed him to develop a 16-page brochure within six weeks. His response shows great skill in diplomacy:

Dear _____:

In response to your letter of March 10, I am prepared to begin work on the promotional brochure. However, I will need to meet with you to determine the following:

1. Definition and purpose of the brochure.
2. Budget and number of brochures you expect to print.
3. Sources of graphic or photographic sections.
4. Subjects to be covered in the text.

I look forward to meeting with you as soon as possible to resolve these issues.

Sincerely,

As expected, the president never responds to this letter. While it is not advisable to delegate assignments back to executives in every case, this was one instance where it was appropriate. If the president did, in fact, want the brochure to be produced, he would have held the meeting and answered the questions.

If you receive a letter demanding a response or giving you an assignment you think should not belong to you, there are several ways you can respond. An angry reply only makes matters worse. The passive tactic—not answering at all—does nothing to resolve the problem. Your best tactic is to take the matter up with your manager, through the normal reporting chain.

One manager received a letter from another department, demanding the creation of a monthly report; she thought such an assignment should come from her own supervisor. She sent a photocopy of the original letter and a carbon copy of her response to her supervisor, and returned the original to the sender, along with her response:

Dear _____:

   Thank you for your letter of November 6, regarding the monthly status report on our division's general expense and budget results.
   I've been instructed to have all outside requests such as yours pre-approved, so I forwarded your request to the vice president of this division for approval. Once I have a go-ahead, I will promptly assist you in your study.

                    Sincerely,

This letter might be taken offensively, but there is not much you can do to prevent that, other than to explain that your action is dictated by policy. You can only hope that if the project is approved, you will be able to mend the situation with continued direct and responsive action.

One thing you must keep in mind: You cannot depend solely on letters and memos—no matter how well written. The written word is only part of the process. Face-to-face meetings and even telephone conversations are more effective, because they allow for interaction. However, you will never escape the need for written communication. Letters bridge the physical separation of the two parties, but more than that, they provide documentation that could be needed later on. View letters as tools for getting a response. If they cause others to act, your letters are having their desired effect.

WORK PROJECT

1. You wrote a memo to another manager requesting information, but you haven't received a reply yet. So you instruct an employee to draft a followup letter under your name. The first draft reads:

Dear _____:

We asked for your department's status report more than two weeks ago, and you have not responded.
We must have the report no later than the end of this week.

Sincerely,

What's wrong with this letter, and how should you rewrite it?

2. Your supervisor instructs you to write a memo to the president reminding him that he's late providing a portion of a monthly committee report. Draft a letter that assertively but politely makes this request.

3. You receive a memo demanding immediate preparation of a departmental report for a six-month budget revision. In the past, your supervisor has handled all budget matters. What is the appropriate response?

3

Edit Your Own Work: Improving the Impression You Make

"Talking is like playing on the harp; there is as much in laying the hand on the strings to stop their vibrations as in twanging them to bring out their music."

—Oliver Wendell Holmes, Sr.

A new employee was given the job of preparing a marketing brochure. He was told the narrative section must be no longer than five pages. He wrote a five-page draft and sent it to the appropriate vice president for review. Several days later, it came back with a note attached: "In the interest of simplifying, I have added four new pages."

No matter how objective you are, it is very difficult to evaluate your own work honestly. You already know that it's much easier to advise employees on how to improve their skills than it is to work on your own flaws. In this chapter we'll look at several techniques for editing your own letters. Always remember that simplicity is preferable to complexity. That's the first step to good writing.

THE DIRECT APPROACH

Simplicity means stating the purpose of your letter as clearly and as quickly as possible. Once you have identified your reader, being direct is much easier. There is no need, for instance, to tell a vice president why a report is being prepared if he already knows the value of internal communication. And the space it takes to include that unnecessary information can be put to better use—to explain deadlines, for example. You can simplify your own letters by eliminating extraneous words. By using the simpler wording, you will significantly improve your letters. The accompanying sidebar demonstrates how you can make these changes.

Keeping your message simple and direct also helps add a friendly tone. This does not mean the letter must be informal, only that it includes a human element. Placing too much distance in your letters adds nothing to them; expressing yourself in a clear and honest form takes nothing away.

Excessive wording often is an attempt to shield uncertainty. Never try to mask a lack of knowledge with fancy phrases. Decide what you want to say, get the information you need, and then express yourself in the simplest, most direct way possible. Extra words in a letter only take up space, emphasize weakness, and detract from your message.

KEEPING TO ONE PAGE

A good rule of thumb for self-editing is to impose a standard on yourself: any communication must be reduced to one page. Of course, there are bound to be exceptions to this rule. Some letters must run longer simply because there's a lot of material to cover. In general, however, you should be able to state a direct message and ask for a response in three or four paragraphs. If you find your letters consistently running more than one page, look for material that can be deleted.

Some letters don't really get to the main point until the second or

---

Before and After

Extraneous Words

Before editing	*After editing*
full and complete	full
at this point in time	now
management personnel	managers
additional changes	changes
complete details	details
it is our intended purpose	we intend
once per month	monthly
main priorities	priorities
we have observed that	we know
estimated results	estimates
12-month period	year
advanced transaction processing	computerized
negative profits	losses

Complex Wording

Before editing	*After editing*
The enclosed report is a full and complete summary of production at this point in time. Management personnel have submitted additional changes and provided complete details for the report. It is our intended purpose to prepare this report once per month.	The enclosed report is a full summary of production as of this month. Managers have submitted changes and details. We intend to prepare this report monthly.
It is our intention to expedite the analysis of relevant statistical trend factors in order to comply with the deadline imposed by management personnel.	We will study the trends as soon as possible so that we can meet the deadline.

---

third paragraph. You might find that your opening is really a warm–up and can be taken out without any loss of meaning. In fact, removing the first paragraph might make your letter more powerful. In some cases, good editing consists of nothing more than elimination. Consider this letter:

Dear _____:

As you know, we have been preparing for month-end closings with a preclosing internal audit. The errors we've found in the past have enabled us to save time in the high-pressure first week of the new month, and to thus get financial statements completed earlier.

Our preclosing audit deadline is upon us again. We will appreciate receiving your department's summary, in the same format as last month's, no later than the 25th.

Please let me know if this deadline creates a hardship for you, and how we can help.

Sincerely,

Now look at the letter again. Try getting rid of the first paragraph altogether. It isn't necessary: The reader, who has been sending in a report each month, knows all about the preclosing audit. The point of the letter doesn't even start until the second paragraph. Whenever you find yourself starting out with the phrase "As you know . . . ," you can probably cut that sentence completely. If the reader already knows it, there's no reason to say it again. In this case, the "as you know" part is the entire opening paragraph.

Good letters are brief. If you find yourself starting out with a simple idea and ending up with a lengthy report, then you're having trouble expressing yourself. Look for the essential message and do away with anything that doesn't add to it.

EIGHT SUGGESTIONS FOR SELF-EDITING

Strengthen your writing skills by practicing these eight practical suggestions, and improve letters your staffers write by establishing the suggestions as standards for good letter writing in your department.

1. Keep it human.

Remember that you are a human writing to another human. There's
nothing wrong with starting out on a friendly note (but don't be too
familiar unless it's appropriate). Your opening should either get right to
the point, or introduce a human element to what you want to communicate.

Compare the following openings and alternatives:

Stiff	*More human*
The deadline for the monthly report is rapidly approaching.	We need your help again. It's monthly report time.
I must once again ask for your participation, along the same lines as last month.	I really appreciated the help you gave me last month. Now I'm back again.
The extra assistance you provided in the recently completed project is deeply appreciated.	Thanks so much for helping out in a crunch on the project we just completed.

2. Define your purpose early.

Many letters progress from beginning to end without really saying what
they're about. You must certainly have received at least one of these.
Either the letter writer isn't sure of the basic messages, or simply doesn't
understand the importance of focus.

Make sure you know both your message and your reader, and
define your purpose quickly—in the opening sentence, if possible.

3. *Make your request directly.*

You write a letter to convey information, make a statement, complain, acknowledge, or ask for something. You request response, explanation, or information. So be sure to clearly state how you expect the reader to follow up.

Ask your question and give a clear idea of what you want. Don't simply explain the situation and expect the recipient to guess. Compare the following statements:

Weak statements	*Strong statements*
We would appreciate receiving an appropriate response from you.	Please respond directly.
Please compile a report in a format you consider most useful for our purposes.	Please prepare your report using the attached sample worksheet.
Any help you are able to provide about production status, cost, and scheduling will be most useful to us.	We need three things: latest production numbers, final costs, and your next month's schedule.

4. *Give the reader a specific deadline.*

If you need a response by a specific date, be sure to include it in your letter. Many letters state what's expected but not when. That's an invitation to not respond.

"As soon as possible" is a poor deadline. Give a day and a date, and be sure to ask for response in an assertive but friendly way. For example, "If this deadline is a problem, please let me know right away." Or "I need this no later than Monday. Let me know what additional information you need from me to make this deadline."

5. *Close on a strong note.*

Just as you need to open a letter by setting the right tone, you also need to close it strongly. An effective way to do this is to end with a repeat of your request: "Can you meet the deadline?" Or you can make an offer: "Let me know what I can do to help."

A sincere and powerful closing makes it hard for the reader to resist what you're asking. But a weak, trailing close can undo whatever good points you raise in the body of the letter. To work, your letter must end powerfully and with a call for action.

Weak endings	*Strong endings*
If you will not be able to meet this deadline, I would appreciate your letting me know.	Please call if there's any deadline problem. Otherwise, I look forward to your response.
We would appreciate any assistance you might be able to provide.	Can you help?
We think the report will be more valuable if you decide to participate in its preparation.	I'm looking forward to working with you on this report.

6. Test content against your message.

Before you send out anything, review your first draft. What is the main message you want to convey? Is there anything in the letter that is not directly related to that message? If so, remove it.

Avoid the pitfall of assuming that your letters must be long in order to carry weight. A short letter that clearly states your purpose and creates a response succeeds by its very simplicity.

7. Look for words you don't need.

Remove modifiers that you don't need. For example, a "monthly period" is really only a "month" and describing someone as a "qualified professional" is redundant. Avoid buzzwords or meaningless phrases such as "truly unique."

Also replace complex words or phrases with simpler ones that work as well. For example, a "preliminary attempt" is nicely expressed as a "first try."

8. Write in the active voice.

Create a tone of positive action in the way you express yourself. The active voice creates a stronger form of expression and eliminates words. Passive expressions portray action as though it is out of your control (something is caused to happen, for example). In comparison, active expressions convey a sense of action, clarify intent and meaning, and put you in control. Ask yourself who or what is acting in the sentence. Do you take actions (the active voice), or are actions performed by you (the passive voice)? For example, compare the passive "The report will be written by me" with the active "I will write a report."

Remember that the essence of communication is getting to the point—telling the other person what you need, when you need it, and why. Sincerity and honesty in your letters will get results. The letter is a way to talk to the recipient; that's all you should be trying to achieve. A direct, simple letter will invariably be better received and responded to than a three-page monologue that never gets around to explaining why you're writing in the first place.

WORK PROJECT

1. Rewrite the following sentences to clarify the message and to remove what could be interpreted as an offensive tone.

    a. You must comply with this request at once.
    b. You are to respond with a full report within one month.
    c. Get back to me as soon as you receive this letter.

2. How could the following phrases be simplified?

    a. Detailed and complete analysis
    b. You must be cognizant of the fact that

c. The current annual period
d. At some future date and time

3. How could the following ending be made stronger?

We intend to complete this project by the end of the current monthly period and hope that your schedule will allow you to submit information by then.

4

Match the Style to the Message: The Major Types of Letters

"I have made this letter longer than usual because I lack the time to make it short."

—Blaise Pascal

A collection notice came into the accounts payable department warning that if the amount due was not paid within ten days, legal action would commence. The amount due was zero. One of the employees wrote to the agency, pointing out that nothing was due, and received back an equally threatening letter. The problem was finally resolved by sending out a check, payable in the amount of zero dollars and zero cents. One last computer-generated letter was received, thanking the company for finally honoring its commitment.

In this age of automation, correspondence often is assigned to a computer. Even letters that are composed by humans can lack the human touch, however. Be aware of why you are writing, and tailor your letters to a specific situation. A form of communication that works well for one reader will not always be appropriate in another setting. The content, tone, level of formality, and the way a message is stated must all be individually designed depending on the purpose of the letter.

SALES LETTERS

We all receive promotional literature, both at home and at work, on a daily basis. But have you ever written a promotion piece? Perhaps not, if you work for a large organization where promotions are developed by specialized departments or outside mail order consulting firms. In a smaller corporation, though, you might be called upon to perform many different functions—including developing a direct-mail letter.

Example: A small management consulting firm in a midwestern city specializes in helping clients find the best automated systems. The city has approximately 100 businesses large enough to be prospective customers. In the past, most new business has come from referrals. The president decides it's time to try a direct-mail approach, and an account manager offers to write a sales letter to introduce the company. It will be followed up with a telephone contact and, if needed, a second letter (see Figure 4-1 for the full process).

This sales campaign is used on a small scale, with only about five letters going out each week. This way, if any information on the prospective customer is available, each letter can be personalized. In one case the first letter reads:

Dear _____:

Don't be typical. You've probably seen a lot of ads for hardware and software. That's how the typical business gets a computer, by responding to an ad. We suggest that you should not make the same mistake.

Once you get a computer, you find out that for all the money spent, no one on your staff knows how to use it, and the operations manuals are little or no help. For the huge investment made, you find you're still a long way from automation.

We are a local, well-managed professional firm with more than 10 years of experience. Our staff of 14 account managers serves as

Figure 4-1.   Sales promotion letters.

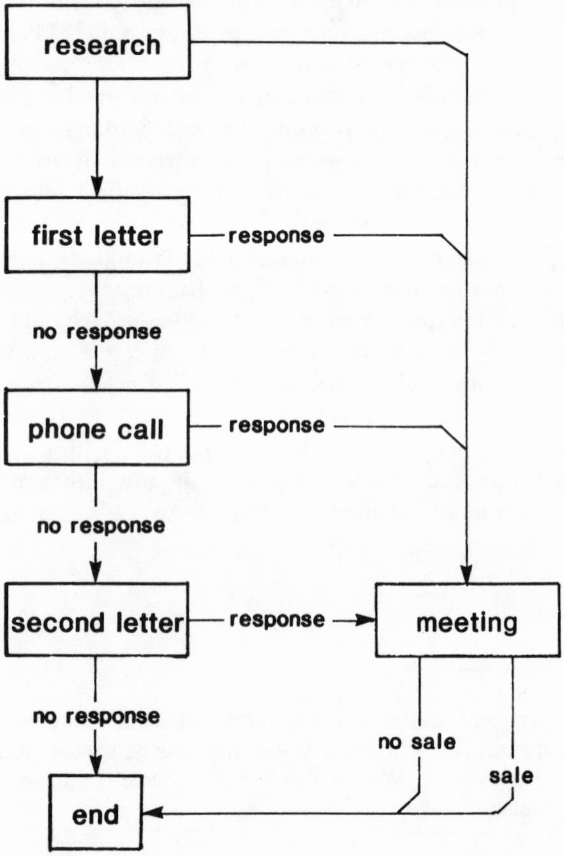

a consulting team specializing in saving money, not merely in finding and installing a computer system.

We don't think a computer should be purchased in the dark. You have had a 553% growth in volume over the past four years, but you still process your sales manually. You can save money with automation, but I suspect that no one has come along yet and shown you how.

We can work with you to find the best alternative, by defining exactly what you need. We are not tied in to any one manufacturer, but work with each client individually. This simple but rare approach has saved money for virtually all our clients.

I'd like to tell you more. Can we get together next week?

Sincerely,

Five days later, the manager follows up with a phone call. Depending on the outcome, one of two letters is then sent. One acknowledges the appointment:

Dear _____:

It was a pleasure to speak with you this morning, and I will visit you in your offices next Tuesday at 10 a.m.

In the meantime, I encourage you to speak with our other clients. I am enclosing a complete list of current companies with whom we work, including contact names and phone numbers.

I am confident that you will be impressed with the level of service we offer, and I look forward to meeting you in person.

Sincerely,

If an appointment is not granted, a different sales letter goes out:

Dear _____:

It was a pleasure to speak with you this morning, and I am sorry
that you will not be able to meet with us in the near future.

I am enclosing a complete list of our current clients, including
contact names and telephone numbers. Please feel free to
contact any of the people of the list in your efforts to find an
affordable computer system.

If we can be of service to you in the future, please call.

Sincerely,

The companies that do not grant an appointment are not dropped from
the list of prospects. Followup letters go out six months later; only after
that second effort is a name dropped.

The sales promotion does not end with the first meeting. Another
letter goes out after the appointment.

Dear _____:

Thank you for meeting with me on Tuesday to discuss your
automation needs. I hope we will be doing business in the future.

I understand that you need to consider our offer and to compare it
with other service providers in the area. I again invite you to
contact our other clients. We believe that continued service and
support are critical in the automation process, and that none of
our competitors can claim the same level of service that we
provide.

We will be looking forward to speaking with you again soon.

Sincerely,

The letters in this case are used to make and maintain contact. Once a prospect becomes a client or customer, the sales and marketing personnel take over.

Here are three important points to remember about the sales promotion letter:

1. The initial contact must be followed up. The letter is only part of the communication process.
2. Before writing a promotional letter, you should have the name (correctly spelled) and title of the right person to contact.
3. Personalize the letter to the company or individual. Do some research to collect financial statistics or industry facts, and incorporate them into your letter. That little extra effort will make your letter stand out.

CUSTOMER RELATIONS

You can spend a lot of time and money promoting your company's products or services, but you must also be able to respond to customers after the sale. An organization that fails in customer service will not be able to maintain its growth.

Real customer service means being able to take action to resolve legitimate complaints. As we've said before, don't make promises unless you can keep them, either directly or by seeing that someone else does. Follow up with another letter or even with a phone call to make sure that the service response you promise is carried through.

Try not to answer a complaint with a standardized, "off-the-shelf" response letter; they are usually far from satisfactory, as this example shows:

Dear _____:

We are in receipt of your letter of January 10 pointing out the poor service response time from our sales department.

It is our policy to ensure as quick a response as possible. Events sometimes prevent our sales personnel from personally address-

ing every request on the same day received. However, we are
committed to the highest quality of service after the sale, and will
continue to promise courteous and prompt service in the future.

We look forward to providing you with a continued high level of
service, and invite you to call upon us for your future needs.

Sincerely,

This letter is impersonal and automatic, and takes up space promoting
the company rather than addressing the complaint. It also fails to resolve
what might be a chronic service and response problem. Here's an
alternative:

[Revised]

Dear _____:

Thank you for your letter of January 10 pointing out the poor
response time and lack of courtesy from our sales department.

I placed a call today to your personal service representative and
asked why the problem occurred. He stated that the day you
called was very hectic, but that the way you were treated was
inappropriate. He has promised to contact you by telephone at
once, to apologize.

In addition, we are reviewing our service supervision procedures
to ensure that incidents such as this do not recur.

We appreciate your letting us know about your problem, as our
commitment to service is one we take seriously. I am certain you
will not have any further problems. However, please contact me if
you are dissatisfied for any reason.

Sincerely,

PROPOSAL LETTERS

You may be called upon to write proposal letters—accompanying your proposal for some action plan—either to someone in your company or to a client. It should include a succinct summary of your proposal and a brief review of the main arguments that support your point of view. In dealing with representatives of another firm, be aware of their sensibilities, especially if you are a consultant and you are telling them something they may not be happy to hear. On the other hand, don't allow polite language to make your argument sound tentative. You want to stand behind your proposal. You have done considerable investigation and your writing is based on your knowledge, experience, and research. Your letter should sound thoughtful, clear, confident, and, of course, well mannered.

Example: A securities firm asks a consultant for a plan to expand its services nationwide. The firm's top executives were eager to bring in a strong wave of new business, but the consultant's research showed that an attempt at rapid growth was likely to be detrimental to the firm in the long term. He proposed a more modest plan, and wrote this letter to accompany his proposal:

Dear _____:

The attached proposal suggests several methods for expanding the company's geographic influence.

The conclusion of our study is that your expansion should be much more gradual than you have indicated. At our initial meeting, you stated that you want sales offices in 45 states within two years. However, initial attempts at creating profitable regional offices have not met with your own expectations.

Some important points to keep in mind when reviewing your expansion goals versus our proposal:

—Most of your competitors have greater financial strength.
—Your major competitors have been in operation for many more years.

—Four other firms offer customers a wider range of products
and service.

Our conclusion does not dispute the higher level of personal
service you and your branch offices provide to customers. On the
contrary, this is your strongest competitive advantage. However, if
you attempt too rapid a plan of expansion, you would have to
sacrifice that service claim. To attain the goal of creating offices in
45 states will require capital and the creation of an administrative
support system that you do not yet have: automated systems for
reporting to remote offices, trained personnel, and the ability to
communicate electronically over hundreds of miles.

After reviewing the attached proposal in detail, you will, I feel
confident, agree with my findings. I look forward to meeting with
you to discuss the steps that must be taken to put the plan into
effect.

Sincerely,

An internal proposal, unlike one from an outsider, will probably contain
more direct knowledge about operations but fewer observations. It
presents a different point of view. Internal proposals may contain ideas
for cutting costs, modifying procedures, or expanding a department.
Cover letters that accompany them should highlight the problem from
an insider's perspective and offer a solution. Costs, savings, and arguments supporting a proposed change should be briefly described in the
letter, then expanded upon in the proposal itself.

Example: One manager prepared a detailed analysis of costs and
concluded that the company could save a great deal of money by moving
her department to a new location. To accompany her proposal to the
vice president, she wrote this cover letter:

Dear _____:

The enclosed proposal recommends that the entire customer
service department be moved to the third floor, from its present
fifth-floor location.

Most of our contact takes place with the marketing department, which is on the third floor. Included in the proposal are several typical examples of the communications lapses that have occurred over the past six months. I believe the majority of these problems could have been eliminated if our departments were closer together.

In addition, recent expansion of our staff size has created a space problem, which further inhibits our efficiency. While there is no room for expansion on the fifth floor, the third floor is more suited to the department's current size.

Major costs of the move include revision of the phone system, moving and rehooking of computer terminals, and time lost during the move itself. We have estimated the total cost at $2,500. However, our projections show that savings resulting from being situated in a more convenient space, while intangible, should far exceed this one-time cost.

I am requesting a meeting with you and the director of marketing to go over this proposal. I have already discussed this idea with her, and she endorses it with enthusiasm. I look forward to your response.

Sincerely,

Preparing a study to support your proposal is a smart idea. If you simply state your request, but offer no backup data, you are less likely to get approval. Whenever you have a suggestion to management, be willing to propose solutions rather than merely present problems. It demonstrates your ability to solve problems, and you're also more likely to get what you ask for.

ASSIGNMENT LETTERS

For successful delegation in your department, you will sometimes find it necessary to document assignments by putting them in writing. It's also a good idea to reinforce them with oral instructions; new managers are often frustrated to learn that employees either misunderstand written assignments or fail to respond. Why? Perhaps the manager was not clear or specific enough. Here's an example:

Dear _____:

We need a procedure to track travel and entertainment expenses and ensure the budget is not exceeded on a monthly basis.

When you have the time, please give me a breakdown by month for the year thus far, showing where actual and budgeted expenses vary.

Sincerely,

This letter is vague on the specifics of the assignment and does not give a deadline; "When you have the time" is not sufficient. To effectively delegate through a letter, you must be more precise. Here's an alternative:

[Revised]

Dear _____:

Please work up a monthly analysis of travel and entertainment expenses year to date, broken down by month. Also prepare a monthly update, showing actual, budget, and variance in the account. A sample worksheet is attached showing the format I would like you to use. If you have any suggestions for an alternative format, I welcome your ideas.

Also note that an explanation of all variances should accompany the report.

I need the year-to-date breakdown by the end of this week, and monthly updates by the fifth of each month. Please let me know at once if these deadlines are a problem. Otherwise, I'll look for the first analysis this Friday.

Sincerely,

Here an exact assignment is given, including deadline, format, and content. The employee is invited to suggest alternatives, and is given the opportunity to come to the manager and explain why the deadline will not be met. In this example, the manager has every reason to expect a successful delegation.

INQUIRY LETTERS

The secret to successful inquiry letters is to ask for specific information. If you expect a meaningful response, be very precise about what you need.

Example: As part of a research project, a manager needs information about the development of a product. He writes to a department head in another city:

Dear _____:

I'm working on a research project for the executive committee in our home office, and need to find out more about the development of your management software products.

I would like to hear from you as soon as possible and will read what you send with interest.

Sincerely,

This letter does not ask for the type of information needed, nor does it include a deadline. If the manager gets a response at all, it is likely to be a brief note describing the product in very general terms. On the second try, he produces this letter:

[Revised]

Dear _____:

I'm working on a research project for the executive committee in the home office, and would like to include information on your management software products.

I understand that you have compiled a developmental cost study, showing the annual expenditures and estimated versus actual recovery periods. Can I get a copy of your study?

The report is due by March 10, so I would appreciate getting the material before then. I'll phone you next week, and I look forward to reading your study.

Thanks for your help.

Sincerely,

Now the letter identifies exactly what the manager needs and when. Promising to follow up with a phone call is a friendly piece of insurance. When the manager does call, it's likely that he'll hear, "I've already put it in the mail."

Make inquiries precise and indicate when you need the information. Also explain the purpose; this avoids misunderstandings, allays any suspicions, and reduces delays.

REJECTION LETTERS

The hardest letters to write are those that say *no*, that turn down employment applications, supplier proposals, or requests from outside your department. You need tact and a sympathetic use of language to soften the bad news you have to write.

Bringing grace and style to rejection letters is a skill worth cultivating. You'll know you are succeeding in this difficult task when you receive thank-you calls or notes in response. But because rejection is difficult, many business letters resort to formal and unfriendly statements. The rejection from publishing companies is typical:

> We appreciate the opportunity to review your book proposal. Regrettably, it is not suitable for us. Good luck placing it elsewhere.

The same is often true with rejections to candidates for jobs. The personnel department may send out a standard rejection notice:

> We have reviewed the candidates for the position we have open, and have selected another individual. We wish you the best of luck finding employment elsewhere.

No one likes to hear they are not wanted, so when you must write a rejection letter, combine a straightforward message with a little sympathy. Suppose you are asked to write a letter to a supplier advising that you have decided to buy from someone else.

> Dear _____:
>
> Thank you for spending the time making your presentation to us last week.
>
> We have completed the difficult task of comparing bids and have decided to place our business with one of your competitors. This is no reflection on the quality of your product, or on your presentation. To the contrary, your professionalism and the high quality and fair pricing of your product made our decision all the more difficult.
>
> Sincerely,

Writing a "friendly" rejection is easy compared to the task of drafting a more critical one. Imagine you must write a rejection letter to a supplier whose product is substandard. Your purpose is to reject the company in such a way that it will stop sending salespeople to your office, and to make it clear you will never buy from them. Here is one possible solution:

Dear _____:

We have made a final decision on the selection of a raw-material supplier and must report that we have decided to place all our business elsewhere.

We are required to apply rigid standards in the selection of materials in our manufacturing process and your product did not meet those specifications.

Your product is probably of excellent quality for companies that manufacture under different circumstances, and we wish you the best of luck in finding those companies.

Sincerely,

LETTERS TO EMPLOYEES

Letters to your staff can be powerful tools to acknowledge a job well done, and equally effective as a way to correct a developing trend.

Everyone likes to be recognized for good work, and a letter or memo of appreciation can mean a great deal to employees. As long as you are sincere and do not use such letters to excess, they can help keep morale and motivation at a high level. For example:

Dear Susan:

You did an exceptional job on the monthly report last week. I know you have not worked on this before, and I appreciated your responding on short notice.

The report was error-free and complete in every detail. I am forwarding a copy of this letter to your personnel file, and to the president of the company as well.

It's always reassuring to a manager to know there are people in the department who can be depended upon to do a professional job.

With sincere thanks,

Critical letters to employees are less fun to write but just as important. You must document any criticisms, not only for the personnel file but also so that the employee has the chance to respond to what you say and to correct the problem. Here's an example:

Dear Frank:

As I have already told you in person, I was not satisfied with the work you did on the monthly report.

I found six math and four spelling errors. I believe these would have been found and corrected if you had taken a little time to double check your work before turning in the report.

From now on, I must insist that you submit draft copies of reports to me before final versions are sent out of the department.

I expected this problem to resolve itself since I first brought it to your attention more than a year ago. Our work reflects on the entire department, and I must insist on the highest possible standards from everyone.

As we have discussed many times, I believe you have the potential to be a valuable employee. But that also depends upon your demonstrated concern with accuracy.

A copy of this letter will be placed in your personnel file.

Sincerely,

Warmth and sincerity are the essense of communication. Even in the most disagreeable letter, you have the opportunity to express your true feelings and to communicate genuinely with a peer, employee, manager, or outsider. Not only does the tone of your letter convey something about you, it also sends out a message about your organization.

You can write a concise letter that clearly states what you want, and still include a human element. Achieving this combination in a natural style is the key to writing the best possible business letters.

WORK PROJECT

1. Your company has sent hundreds of promotional letters over the past year but has received very little response. What type of follow-up do you suggest to improve this record?

2. A customer writes an angry letter to you, complaining about a rude employee. How should you respond, and what other actions will you take?

3. You are frustrated that employees in your department do not complete assignments you give them, and you wonder if your instructions are inadequate. List several features that should be included in an assignment memo.

5

Identify the Sections:
The Four Parts of
Your Letter

"There is no lighter burden, nor more agreeable, than a pen."

—Petrarch

An employee asked his supervisor for help in writing a letter. "I already have a good middle paragraph," he said, "all I need now is a strong opening."

The supervisor suggested that he begin by stating the purpose of the letter. The employee thought a moment, then asked, "And what would that be?"

You can create a strong, well-organized letter only if you understand why you are writing it in the first place. Many a letter has been drafted without this essential first step, and that only makes the task of writing more difficult than it should be.

There's nothing more satisfying than firmly transforming your thoughts to paper in a manner that holds the reader's attention, communicates clearly what you mean, and leads to the reaction you desire. That's power. And it can be yours if you define and state your purpose, expand upon it, describe what you want, and ask for the appropriate response.

To achieve this power, organize your thoughts along the lines of the letter, recognizing that every letter contains four parts: opening, expansion, action, and closing (see Figure 5-1). In this chapter, we describe and give examples of these four parts. In reality, not all letters are organized in that order. In a sales letter, for example, your opening might appear on the envelope and your closing can be included as a postscript. But in general, most business letters will follow the format we present in this chapter.

THE FOUR PARTS

When you have read letters that impressed you, chances are that the writer's thinking was clear and the organization of thought was transferred to an organization of sections.

Each part of a letter has a distinct purpose. Each part builds to a complete expression of what you want from the recipient. You can't expand on an idea until you have described that idea in its basic form. And you can't ask for action until the reader knows what you're asking for. A clear communication is a complete one.

Opening

The way you start your letter defines what you're asking, and also determines whether or not the reader will respond. Your opening should achieve two things. It must attract attention, telling the reader in a compelling manner why the message is important. Second, it sets the tone for the rest of the letter.

Getting attention does not mean using startling or offensive language. You are, after all, attempting to convey an important message in a business situation. Be aware of the difference between unnecessary dramatics and earnest communication of an idea.

Setting the tone of a letter is an equally important function of your opening. If you need the help of another department head, you could begin a letter by saying, "I'm working on a job and need to audit your files. Let me know when I can come by." But this is likely to intimidate

Figure 5-1. Parts of the letter.

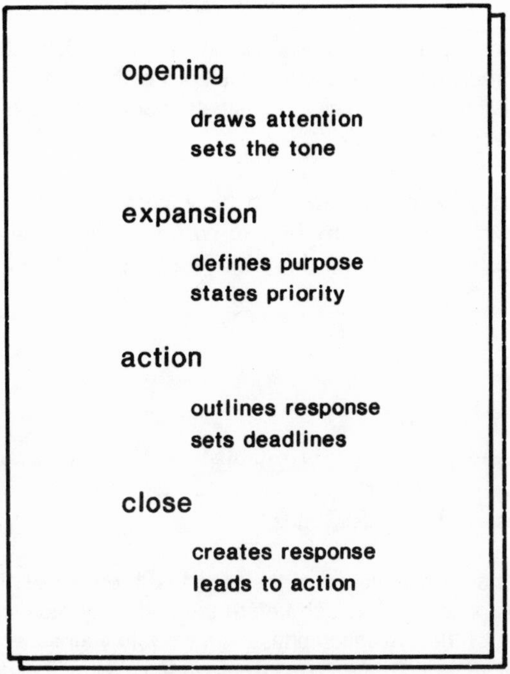

opening

>   **draws attention**
>   **sets the tone**

expansion

>   **defines purpose**
>   **states priority**

action

>   **outlines response**
>   **sets deadlines**

close

>   **creates response**
>   **leads to action**

the reader. You'll set a better tone—and get better results—if you start out with "I need your help. I've been given an assignment that requires background, and would like to visit with you early next week."

Expansion

The second paragraph more thoroughly spells out the purpose, which grows from what you introduce in your opening. It also establishes the priority of your message.

Let's continue with the same example. You have set the tone and told the reader you need to review files. Now you need to describe exactly what you need.

> The project depends upon historical summaries of production for the last three years. Before writing the body of the report, I need to gather this critical information. I estimate that I'll need a full day's review of your files.

This is reassuring, because you describe what you need and why you need it. You're taking away any hint of an investigation, and telling the reader why you're interested in his files. You're establishing your priority.

Action

The purpose and priorities you establish in the expansion paragraph complete the definition of the task at hand. Next you need to outline the desired response and set a deadline.

> My deadline for completion of the report is three weeks. I would like to complete my research before the middle of next week, to allow time for the evaluation phase. If it fits with your schedule, I'd like to visit your department next week on Monday or Tuesday.

Here, you've described exactly what you want to do and when. The reader can now respond that one of those days will work out, and invite you to come by. You have also described your own deadline situation, so that the reader understands why this phase is so urgent to you.

Closing

Never close your letter passively. Ask for a response that's both specific and timely. Your close must cause the reader to grant your request or explain why that's not possible.

> I appreciate any help you can offer to complete this project. Can you let me know before Friday which day will work best for you?

If you don't get a response by Friday, you can call the other manager. But you probably won't have to.

The point here is that a well-constructed letter does not lead to misunderstandings, make the reader feel threatened in any way, or leave questions unanswered. The communication is complete and it calls for a response. That's a successful business letter, one that achieves all its objectives. The message is stated clearly and in a direct but friendly tone, and the recipient is compelled to give you what you ask.

THE OPENING PARAGRAPH

Your letter must start out by quickly stating either the purpose of the letter or a key fact that will attract the reader's interest. In a business communication, you should want to get down to business right away. In a sales letter that is intended to interest the reader in buying what your company offers, you must get and hold the reader's attention. But that is true for every letter you write, because whenever you ask for a response, you are selling. Whether it's a request for information, a complaint letter, or an answer to someone else's original request, you must sell your own point of view.

The opening is the most difficult part to write. Some find it easier to draft the entire letter and then go back and revise the opening paragraph. Another technique is to force yourself to focus and define your letter before you even begin to write, so that you start with the opening and then proceed.

Even a well-defined letter may not work with the first opening paragraph you devise. In that case, go back and change it. Your focus and emphasis may change as you write the letter itself.

Example: A manager in a computer consulting firm receives a letter from a potential customer asking for information about software products and how the firm helps its clients during the automation process. First, the manager drafts this opening:

Dear _____:

Thank you for your letter of March 18. We offer a range of services that you will find very interesting, based upon the issues you raised,

and we'd like to set up an appointment at your convenience to discuss this with you.

By the time the manager finishes writing the letter, he realizes the emphasis is wrong; the idea of asking for an appointment belongs at the end of the letter. But there's another problem with opening: It doesn't address the reader's concerns, so why should he be interested in reading on?

Remember, this manager has received an inquiry from a potential customer, so he should respond from a sales point of view. Professional services must be sold not directly but sympathetically. The writer has expressed apprehension about getting into computers, and that is the key to the appropriate response. The manager redrafts the opening to read as follows:

Dear _____ :

You are absolutely right. Automation is a difficult and intimidating process, and the problems you mentioned in your March 18 letter are precisely the issues we solve for our clients.

In this opening, the manager identifies with the potential customer, hints at a solution, which can follow in the next paragraph, and supports the reader's obvious desire to find reassurance.

Always look for a strong "hook," an opening that immediately gets the reader's attention. In mass mailings, blatant hooks are common: "special offer enclosed" or "a rare opportunity for big savings." In a professional letter, the hook should be subtle. If you offer professional services and are trying to attract a client, you must temper your hook with dignity and sincerity. The computer consulting firm could take a number of different marketing approaches:

Saving money

Have you estimated the cost of automating? If you have, and if you are typical, you'll end up spending two to three times what you estimate, and getting a working system will take a year longer than you think. But it doesn't have to be that way. With a little planning, you can beat the averages.

Alternative to purchase

You want to automate, but can't afford to invest thousands of dollars in hardware. We'd like to tell you how you can achieve full automation without taking that risk, with our practical and low-cost time-sharing plan.

Remote communications

Most people think of a computer just for number crunching. But a company like yours, with a number of offices around the country, also needs an instant, affordable networking system. We'd like to show you how our communications programs work.

These are just examples. Sales can take many forms, and the right opening should depend on the product or service you offer, the type of customer you serve, and how you decide to approach your market.

The opening in a business letter should identify with the reader, state the purpose clearly, and set a positive tone. Remember that every letter you write is an attempt to sell something. Getting a fellow manager to cooperate with you on a project requires selling; so does asking for information from an outside source, reprimanding an employee, complaining about poor treatment, or even acknowledging a good job.

THE EXPANSION PARAGRAPH

Once you draw the reader's attention and set the tone in the opening, the next step is to expand upon your message. That means defining your purpose and setting a priority. Expanding on the opening is nothing more than carrying forward the idea you have introduced and defining it precisely.

Earlier we showed three different approaches to selling automation services. Here's how the expansion sections might read in each of those approaches:

Saving money

The solution is to approach the complex issue of automating by first defining what you need. That's where most businesses

run into problems. They don't take the time to plan out their move
to a computer. We can show you how to outline your own priorities, establish a time and cost budget, and stay within it. More to
the point, we can make the job of automating efficient, practical,
and affordable.

Alternative to purchase

Most people start out buying expensive hardware and software.
But they often discover that the system they purchased isn't right
for them. Time sharing is the best way to explore automation
without having to buy a computer. Everything you need is rented
on a month-to-month basis, and you can cancel the agreement at
any time with only a 30-day notice.

There's no investment of money up front. You pay only for
what you actually use, and we work with you to develop your own
programs. We also train your staff and lead you through every
step on the way to full and successful automation.

Remote communications

As specialists in this field, we have installed networking systems
for more than 50 companies. We work with you in your home
office, and also train personnel in branch offices, ensuring that
instant communications are put into place and are in working
order. We'd like to start out by referring you to some of our other
clients, so that you can see networking in action.

Notice how each of these expansion paragraphs carries the theme from
the opening and explains the value of the company's services from the
three perspectives.

These are purely sales letters, of course, but you can apply the same
idea in any type of letter you write. When you ask another department
head for help, when you assign a job to an employee, and when you
complain to a supplier, you expand upon the theme and tone set in your
opening paragraph.

Where do business letters fail? One common problem is lack of
clear focus on the primary message. The expansion section must continue the established theme, or the reader becomes confused and loses
interest.

Example: This poorly focused response letter to a customer intro-
duces an idea and then expands in an unexpected direction.

Dear _____:

I am very concerned to hear that our field representative did not return your call. We are, of course, most concerned with the quality of service our employees provide.

Along those lines, it might interest you to know that we are now offering an upgrade of the system you purchased last year. For a very minor additional cost, it's now possible to expand your internal memory by three times its present size. I am taking the liberty of calling your sales representative and suggesting he phone you to discuss your new upgrade, in addition to finally getting back to you from last week.

Sincerely,

A response to a customer's complaint letter is surely not the best opportunity to promote new services or products. The letter should be focused on one issue only—resolving the problem. In this case, the manager misses that point altogether. He shouldn't be surprised if the customer's reaction is anger—the opposite of what he wants to achieve. Here's a better approach:

[Revised]

Dear _____:

I am very concerned to hear that our field representative did not return your call. We are, of course, most concerned with the quality of service our employees provide.

Your complaint is a legitimate one, and you have every right to expect a prompt and courteous response. I have placed a call to your representative and instructed him to contact you at once, and to resolve this problem to your complete satisfaction. If for any reason you are not satisfied after he does contact you, please call me collect at the number above.

Sincerely,

This second version is focused completely on the solitary issue of the customer complaint. The expansion paragraph describes the steps that have been taken to resolve the problem and does not deviate from that theme. Of course, if the sales representative is professional and capable, he will be able to satisfy the customer *and* bring up the new line of products. But that's not the issue here, and should not be included in the letter.

Keep a perspective on your reasons for writing. If you have two conflicting messages to convey, write two separate letters. Stay on the subject and address that subject appropriately. The best letters are not cluttered with unrelated thoughts, but deal with the primary issue at hand.

THE ACTION PARAGRAPH

Now that you have opened the letter and expanded upon what you are communicating, it's time to specify the action or reaction you expect. This paragraph outlines either the response you want to get or the actions you promise to take. It also sets a deadline.

The action paragraph of a sales letter should compel the recipient to respond. Let's continue with our three approaches to selling automation services.

Saving money

We're offering a free initial consultation to show you how we work. By the end of that first meeting, you'll see how we can remove the complexity from automation, and save you a great deal of effort and money at the same time. We'd like to meet with you this week.

Alternative to purchase

There's virtually no risk to you in using our time-sharing services. Our agreements run from month to month and can be cancelled at any time. But our experience has shown us that most people get so much value from what we offer that our turnover is quite low. We'd like to arrange an appointment to tell you more at your convenience, preferably next week.

Remote communications

If you have already looked into the cost of installing a networking capability, you will be surprised at the low cost of our system. We can show you how it works with a free orientation meeting in our offices. We can schedule you in for next Thursday, if that's a good date for you.

These paragraphs tie up the presentation by keying in on a critical point. In the first letter, you tell the reader it isn't as complex or expensive as he thought, and you would like to prove it. In the second, you dispose of risk and commitment fears. And in the third, you offer to show how your system is more practical and affordable than the competition.

The action paragraph makes promises (especially in a sales letter) or asks for a specific action. For example, in a letter giving an employee an assignment, you would specify what is to be done and give a precise deadline. Note that in all three examples, time frame is included. That's an action point. Whether you want to get an action decision this week, next week, or this month, be sure to include that deadline in your action section.

THE CLOSING PARAGRAPH

The final part of your letter, the closing, should ask for a direct response or promise specific action. The well-written close will lead to action.

In a letter where you promise to act in some way, the closing summarizes what you will do. A response to a customer complaint, for example, could close like this:

I will personally speak with someone in the sales division this morning and see to it that your request is met. The replacement will be in the mail today.

When you make an assignment to an employee, close with a request for full compliance or immediate communciation:

> Can you complete the report by Tuesday? If not, please see me right away. Otherwise, I'll look forward to receiving your work.

Keep in mind that the close should prompt action. Let's go back to the example of the three sales letters.

Saving money

> Getting in touch with us could save you a great deal of money. Are you interested?

Alternative to purchase

> This alternative to buying expensive hardware and software simply makes sense, and we invite you to find out more. Would you like to get together?

Remote communications

> We can have your complete network up and running within less than one year. Do you want to know more?

Each of these examples ends with a question, which is one way to prompt a response. Questions can be especially effective in a sales letter, but they also work in other situations. When asking another manager for information or giving an assignment by letter, you can end with "Can you make this deadline?" or "Can you call me right away?" Both are good, strong endings that call for a definite response. Another very effective way to close is with a postscript. Here are two samples:

> We would like to meet with you next Monday to show you more. Is that a good day for you?
>
> Sincerely,
>
> P.S. Our first hour's consultation is free.

Or:

> We are offering one hour of free consultation, and would like to arrange a convenient appointment for you.
>
> Sincerely,
>
> P.S. Are you free to meet next Monday?

The postscript, if used correctly, can be the most important part of your letter, because it stands out. Chances are, the reader will look at the postscript before anything else. So if you have a particular point to emphasize, consider putting it in that form.

Example: You are giving a written assignment to an employee who has not met deadlines in the past. Rather than emphasize this negative point in the letter, put a note in the form of a postscript:

> I need this work no later than this Friday. Will you be able to finish it by then?
>
> Sincerely,
>
> P.S. If you expect a problem with the deadline, call me at once.

Here, you have added emphasis without making any negative remarks. That's an effective use of the postscript closing, which can also be thought of as a reinforcement of the letter itself.

CONTINUITY IN YOUR LETTER

A good business letter flows naturally from one point to another, held together with a single focus and primary theme (see Figure 5-2). The tone is consistent, the flow of communication is clear, and all parts fit together to express your meaning in unmistakable terms.

The opening and the closing should identify the key issue. For example, in a sales letter you might mention cost savings or reduction of

Figure 5-2.   Continuity of the letter.

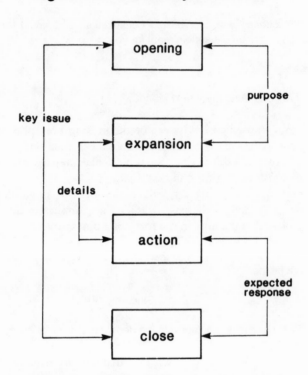

risk in both places. Or you emphasize the critical need to meet a deadline in the opening and closing of an assignment letter.

The purpose of the letter is introduced and clarified in the opening and the expansion paragraphs. All necessary details are filled in by the expansion and action paragraphs. And the expected response (or promised action) is stated in the action and the close.

The relationship between sections cannot be overlooked or ignored. Each statement you make in one paragraph should lead naturally to the next, where it is either expanded upon or concluded. For example:

Opening	I need your help.
Expansion	I've been assigned a report, and I need information you have.
Action	I have a deadline for getting this information, and I need it for the last three years.
Closing	Can you help?

In all your written communications, the key to good writing is structure and organization. The better you know what you're trying to say and the more you understand how your words will be perceived, the better you become at writing effective letters.

The responses you receive are the best measure of your success as a letter writer. If you can write to eliminate misunderstandings, if you see an improvement in action and reaction, then you know you're on the right track.

WORK PROJECT

1. You are preparing a response letter to an angry customer and must apologize for poor service in a field office. There is an obvious problem in supervision of service representatives. Write an opening paragraph that clearly sets the appropriate tone for your letter.

2. List three ways you can promise in your action paragraph to solve the customer's problem, correct the shortcoming in procedures, and ensure that subordinates follow up on your requests.

3. Develop three closing questions for a sales letter that will help prompt a positive response.

6

Construct Effective Letters: Mastering the Art of Writing

"I was thrown out of college for cheating on the metaphysics exam. I looked into the soul of the boy next to me."

—Woody Allen

"Can you help me?" the new clerk asked her manager. "I'm having a problem starting this letter to the vice president of our western division."

The manager suggested trying to understand the letter's message from the reader's point of view. "Figure out how he thinks, what motivates him. Then the solution will come to you."

"Thanks for the advice. But for now, I'm still trying to find his address."

Writing an effective letter is like participating in a dialogue. You say something that creates a response, and then you respond to the other person. The difference is that the other participant in your dialogue— your reader—is not there when you compose your side of the discussion.

Build your letter with the reader's response in mind. List the key points you want to make, and then list the expected responses the reader will have. For example:

Key point	*Responses*
Definition: the task at hand.	Why are you asking me?
You have done this job in the past.	How soon do you need this work?
Our deadline is February 16. But we'd like to receive the final copy by January 31.	That's too soon. I couldn't possibly finish this job by that deadline.
We'd like to meet with you next week.	I won't have time to get together.
We will have to alter our production schedule.	That means it will be my fault if the report doesn't come out on time.
When can we meet?	Next week.

Notice that the process is like a dialogue. You present a request; the recipient (you assume) raises an argument; you address that issue in the next sentence of the letter. Each possible objection is handled and eliminated, so you end up getting what you asked for in the first place.

Example: You are preparing year-end budgets and need information from all departments to complete the job on time. Your first-draft memo to the marketing department reads:

Dear _____:

    Enclosed are worksheets for the year's budget.
    We have filled in this year's results through November 30, for your reference. Please be sure to return the completed budgets to me no later than December 15.

Sincerely,

The marketing department might be too busy to meet the deadline, or might need additional information before it can proceed. If you are aware

of these possible responses, you can anticipate them and solve the
problems in the memo itself:

[Revised]

Dear _____:

   Enclosed are worksheets for the year's budget.
   Our deadline for response is December 15. If there is a
problem with this deadline, please let me know as soon as
possible. I can supply you with additional information if needed, or
assign one of my employees to work with you in completing your
department's budget.
   Let me know how I can help.

                              Sincerely,

Admittedly, this is a simplified example, and you are obviously guessing
at the objections the recipient might raise. But using the process helps
you to organize your letter and enables you to field arguments that are
likely to arise. That's better than simply asking for what you need and
hoping for the best. By eliminating the arguments you consider most
likely, you improve your chances for a positive answer.

   Depending on your own style and your ease with the subject, you
might prefer to draft a first version of the letter and then edit it with an
eye to possible reactions. Or you might find it easier to organize your
thoughts and the format of the message first and then write from your
notes.

   You can never fully anticipate how someone else will interpret your
letter, especially when you're asking for help or making an assignment.
So the best you can hope for is that your message will not create any
misunderstandings and that the possible arguments will be defused in
your final draft.

LETTERS THAT FLOW SMOOTHLY

A well-written letter does not draw attention to itself. The best writing is so natural and clear that the reader doesn't even think about it. The message is understood, the response is obvious, and action is taken. Only poorly written letters draw attention to themselves. You may not be able to explain just *why* one is poor—only that it's difficult to understand.

You must pay close attention to the tone of your letters. You must strive for simplicity and clarity of the message. Both affect the way your message will be comprehended. But your letters must also contain a natural flow. That requires balance and transitions between thoughts.

Here's an assignment letter written without that natural flow:

Dear _____:

I'd like you to prepare an analysis of travel and entertainment expenses in the marketing department for the current year to date.

You did a similar report about six months ago. Please use the same format this time.

Compare the unfavorable variance in the account with the favorable variance in income forecast, and determine whether travel and entertainment is in line with that difference.

We might conclude that the variance is acceptable, given the higher volume of sales, and that the budget should be revised.

Can you get this to me by the end of the week? If that's a problem, please let me know right away.

Sincerely,

While this letter clearly defines what you need, it lurches from one paragraph to the other without a smooth transition. Conversational letters are easier to read. Be aware of the need for a change in emphasis or thought. A redrafted version:

[Revised]

Dear _____:

Can you prepare an analysis of travel and entertainment expenses in the marketing department for the current year to date?

Please use the same format for this report that you devised six months ago, with one change: We need to compare this unfavorable variance with the favorable variance in the year-to-date income forecast.

We might conclude that the travel and entertainment variance is not unreasonable, given our sales volume, and that the budget should be revised.

I recognize that this additional analysis means more time, but can you get the report to me by the end of the week? If that's a problem, please let me know right away.

Sincerely,

The changes are minor and subtle. The letter is about the same length as the first version, but it reads more easily and the exact assignment is clearer. What are the transition points?

Paragraph	Transition
1	prepare an analysis
2	use the same format
2	We need to compare
3	We might conclude
3	budget should be revised
4	means more time

Notice now that the focus of thought moves through the letter in a single line. If you read just the transitional phrases by themselves, you can see that thought clearly.

Forcing yourself to think in terms of transitions will add a thread of focus throughout your letters and will keep you on track. If you have more than one idea to convey, there is always a way to make a smooth transition, although that might take more creative effort than going from one step to another in a single idea.

Example: You write to an employee, describing an assignment; you also want to emphasize the importance of getting the work done by your deadline. You could describe what you want in one paragraph, end that paragraph, and then state:

> I must have this within two weeks. If you will not be able to meet that deadline, let me know.

But if you use a transition, you can strengthen the thought:

> With that description, you should be able to proceed at once. The two-week deadline is critical. So if you have any questions, please come and see me right away.

Transitions do not have to occur from the end of one paragraph to the beginning of another, although that is the most obvious form. The important thing is that the primary thought of one section carries over to the next.

Remember your primary message, and stay with that message throughout your letter. Adding a strong transition between paragraphs strengthens and clarifies your thought. That technique, combined with your understanding of the recipient's point of view, will make your letters effective and powerful communication tools.

WORK PROJECT

1. What problems might you encounter when asking for information from:

    a. The president of the company?
    b. A fellow department manager?
    c. An employee?

2. Your letter requesting information from another department gets an angry response. How can you correct the misunderstanding?

3. Construct three possible transitions for a letter that makes two unrelated requests: one for historical sales information and the other for a preliminary sales forecast.

7

Pay Attention to Details: Keys to Professional Communication

"Get your facts first, then you can distort them as you please."

—Mark Twain

A manager was considering a candidate from another department for a job opening. The position called for a good deal of writing, so the manager sent a note to the candidate's department head, asking whether he was qualified. A memo came back with the comment, "He is capable of doing the job you described, but be prepared to check work carefully before sending it out. His speling is atrosious."

Some of the little things about letters—spelling, neatness, format, and overall appearance—are sometimes considered unimportant details. They are details, but they are not unimportant. In fact, collectively they create the impression you make on someone else. Just as the message behind the words conveys your thoughts, those little details tell the reader what kind of person you are.

Make it a rule that any written communication from your department must be as correct as possible. Inspire your employees with the attitude of pride and care. You will probably have to monitor letters as they are prepared to make sure your standards are being followed. As new employees come into your department, or when temporary helpers work there, you will have to reiterate your standards and ensure compliance. Even employees who already know the rules for good letters will lapse occasionally. While you should not have to review every letter employees prepare, you should maintain a reasonable level of direct supervision. Check periodically to make sure letters conform to your minimum standards.

SECTIONS OF THE LETTER

In Chapter 5, we discussed and examined the four major parts in the body of the letter: the opening, expansion, action, and closing paragraphs. But business letters contain other elements as well, and all writers must be careful in using them. Set standards for uniformity for all employees. The following rules will help you to instruct staff members in the proper format for business letters.

Date

The most common format for writing a date is month, day, and year:

August 15, 1988

In your business letters, do not abbreviate the month. It should be written out in full, without exception. The day is always followed by a comma. In some internal reports or on worksheets, abbreviations are appropriate. Acceptable forms are:

Aug. 15, 1988

8-15-88

8/15/88

None of these can be used for the business letter, however.

An alternate form for dates places the day first:

15 August 1988

This format is commonly used in the military and is the standard method in European countries. It has two advantages: It eliminates the need for a comma, and it simplifies clerical work when a numerical filing system is used.

Name and Address

In every letter you write, take extra care to spell the recipient's name correctly. Nothing will get you off to a bad start faster than misspelling someone's name. If you do not have a letter or a business card from the person, call the company to determine the exact spelling and title.

The address block should start with the individual's name and title. Take either one or two lines, depending on the length of the title. Two examples:

Mr. Harold Green, President

Ms. Melanie Smith
Executive Vice President, Operations

Follow this with the company name. Don't use abbreviations unless the abbreviation is part of the name itself. For example, if a company's name is "HG Enterprises, Inc., " it is wrong to spell out Incorporated.

Next comes the address. When a floor or suite number is included, you can write it in one of two ways:

4215 Atlantic Blvd., Suite 618

Suite 618
4215 Atlantic Blvd.

Conclude with city, state, and zip code, all on one line. The state abbreviation system favored by the U.S. Postal Service—two capital letters, no commas—is the easiest to use; see accompanying chart.

Official Post Office Abbreviations for U.S. States and Canadian Provinces

Alabama	AL	North Carolina	NC
Alaska	AK	North Dakota	ND
Arizona	AZ	Ohio	OH
Arkansas	AR	Oklahoma	OK
California	CA	Oregon	OR
Colorado	CO	Pennsylvania	PA
Connecticut	CT	Rhode Island	RI
Delaware	DE	South Carolina	SC
Florida	FL	South Dakota	SD
Georgia	GA	Tennessee	TN
Hawaii	HI	Texas	TX
Idaho	ID	Utah	UT
Illinois	IL	Vermont	VT
Indiana	IN	Virginia	VA
Iowa	IA	Washington	WA
Kansas	KS	West Virginia	WV
Kentucky	KY	Wisconsin	WI
Louisiana	LA	Wyoming	WY
Maine	ME		
Maryland	MD	Alberta	AB
Massachusetts	MA	British Columbia	BC
Michigan	MI	Labrador	LB
Minnesota	MN	Manitoba	MB
Mississippi	MS	New Brunswick	NB
Missouri	MO	Newfoundland	NF
Montana	MT	Northwest Territories	NT
Nebraska	NE	Nova Scotia	NS
Nevada	NV	Ontario	ON
New Hampshire	NH	Prince Edward Island	PE
New Jersey	NJ	Quebec	PQ
New Mexico	NM	Saskatchewan	SK
New York	NY	Yukon	YT

Subject

In some instances, you will want to make reference to the subject of a letter before you get into the actual body. This subject line should be written after the full address but before the salutation; double space before and after. Most subjects involve only one typed line, although two or three can be used when necessary:

> Subject: Shipment of March 24, 1988
>
> Invoice 14762, dated 3/24/88
> Identification number 34905-6873-88

If your reader has a high volume of correspondence going back and forth with people in your company, specifying the subject provides a quick orientation.

Salutation

A letter usually begins with the word "Dear" and then names the person being written to. In most business correspondence to someone you have not met, the greeting should include the appropriate title, such as Mr., Mrs., Miss, or Ms. Today the "Ms." greeting is coming into popular use regardless of marital status. Certainly if you do not know that status, using "Ms." is the best alternative. If some other title is appropriate for the person you're writing to (such as Dr., Hon., The Rev.), make sure you know the proper title before addressing your letter.

What should you do if you're not certain whether the individual is a man or a woman? Suppose you are answering a letter from M. Smith or Pat Jones. You might try to make a guess based on a signature, but you could easily guess wrong. Your best bet is to address your letter as follows:

> Dear M. Smth:
>
> Dear Pat Jones:

This is not the most comfortable way to begin a letter, but it's preferable to risking offending someone. Note that in business letter format, the salutation is followed by a colon.

When is it appropriate to use first names? In some sectors of business, first names are used in the second communication, possibly even in the first. Salespeople, for instance, tend to use first names more freely than most. Or, as H. L. Mencken put it, "The first Rotarian was the first man to call John the Baptist 'Jack.' "

Overly familiar styles can alienate or even insult a recipient. As a general rule, address someone senior in rank in your organization by the more formal Mr. or Mrs. When communicating with a peer or subordinate, use last names until you have established personal contact.

If a reply to your first letter is addressed to you by first name, then you should reply in kind. And if the person signs her letter "Sandra" rather than "Sandra Smith," take that as a signal that first names are now appropriate.

With someone you consider a peer, it is reasonable to assume that first names should be used. But when in doubt, stay with the formal "Dear Mr. _____" or "Dear Ms. _____." There is one exception: If you are trying to add a personal or friendly tone to your communication, the informal first-name salutation helps.

The Body of the Letter

After the date, name and address, subject (if needed), and salutation, begin your letter. Be aware of the need for all four parts:

1. Opening
2. Expansion
3. Action
4. Closing

It is not always necessary to break your letter into four parts, and not every type of letter needs these absolute distinctions. But use this sequence in your thought process as you plan your communication. Keeping these four parts in mind helps reduce any unneeded parts from your letter. Remember, your objective is to keep the communication to one page whenever possible.

Compliment

This is the first line of the signature block, followed by three or four spaces for your signature.

There are a wide range of compliments, some more formal than others. Some examples of formal compliments:

> **Respectfully,**
> **Very respectfully,**
> **Sincerely,**
> **Sincerely yours,**
> **Yours sincerely,**

Informal compliments include:

> **Best wishes,**
> **As always,**
> **Your friend,**

Note that the first word of the compliment is capitalized and the second is not. The compliment ends with a comma.

There is no hard-and-fast rule about what you should include as a compliment. In an informal letter, use whatever wording is comfortable, given the degree of your personal contact with the recipient.

Be sure to maintain the same level of formality in both salutation and compliment forms. For example, if you address the letter to "Mr. Harold Green," don't end with "Best wishes." And if you start out "Dear Harold:" don't end with a formal compliment.

Signature, Name, and Title

In most business letters—that is, all but the most informal ones—type in your entire name. Place your title on the line beneath:

> **Sincerely yours,**
>
> **Marilyn C. Kinders**
> **General Manager**

In a formal letter, you should sign your name exactly the same way it is typed underneath: Ms. Kinders would write "Marilyn C. Kinders." But in a less-than-formal letter, it is acceptable to use just the first name in the signature; the full name is still typed.

Identification Initials

If the letter is typed for you by someone else, the typist usually skips either one or two lines and puts in the identification block. The practice of using initials is declining, as word processing provides other, easier ways to identify the actual typist.

In most instances where initials are used, the name of the person signing the letter is placed in capitals, followed by a colon or slant mark, and the typist's initials in lowercase letters.

MCK:prt

MCK/prt

Enclosures

When you include additional materials, a notation of enclosure is added. The purpose is to call the reader's attention to the enclosure and to provide a kind of safety net should the enclosures be inadvertently omitted. The notation itself can be spelled out or abbreviated. For example, if you place a contract in with your letter, you could add:

Enclosure: contract

Encl: two copies, contract

Enc: contract original and copy

If there is more than one enclosure, list each one, using bracketed numbers:

Enclosures: [1] original contract
           [2] list of other clients
           [3] current brochure

Copies

If you send copies of your letters to other people, list their names at the end of the letter, with the abbreviation "cc:"

cc: John Markham
    Susan Billings

The "carbon copy" note at the bottom of a letter is intended to let your reader know who else has received a copy. This is not only a matter of courtesy, but also a way to maintain a complete line of communication. It creates a record of who has been advised of a situation and who knows about past issues, requests, or problems. The notation is used for other purposes, too, some of which are political.

Example: A manager writes to a supplier's purchasing agent to complain about slow deliveries. He forwards the letter with a "cc" to the president of the supply company.

The recipient is advised by this notation that the president knows about the complaint. That's a form of communication. In fact, the manager may not send a copy to the president, and the "cc" is included only to exert pressure. The purchasing agent will be more likely to respond immediately and solve the problem mentioned in the complaint, because the president might inquire about what's being done.

Another use of the "cc" can involve an attempt to advance a cause or to make a self-serving statement.

Example: An employee receives a phone call from a division office telling him that a monthly sales report was never received. The employee immediately sends out the information with a cover letter. The letter states that the information was previously sent and must have been lost in the mail. A "cc" of the letter is sent to the employee's supervisor.

The employee does not want people to think that he forgot to send out the monthly information. This letter supposedly defuses that accusation if the division office does complain to the supervisor. So in this case, the letter is self-serving.

Example: Two employees discuss ideas for making a procedure work more efficiently. One has an idea that will save the company thousands of dollars every year. The other drafts a memo to his supervisor, proposing the idea as his own. He also sends a "cc" to the vice president of the division. The second employee has taken credit for someone else's idea and is also trying to gain recognition further up the chain of command.

Some people will intentionally exclude others from a distribution list. This may send the message that the person is somehow not worthy of being included and can be a political statement.

Taking credit for other people's ideas, attempting to advance at someone else's expense, and intentionally leaving people out of distribution are all unprofessional and harmful acts. Unfortunately, such practices do occur. In some companies, political games are widespread, and a lot of energy and time are wasted devising moves or defending against the moves of others. Some people do move ahead in an organization by these means, but most only hurt their own careers and their organization in the long run.

The blind carbon copy, or "bcc," is used when a copy of a letter or memo is sent to a third party without the primary recipient's knowledge.

Example: You are having a problem dealing with the head of a division office, and discuss the situation with another manager, who gives you some ideas of how to respond. As a courtesy, you "bcc" the other manager when you send out your letter.

Use "cc" and "bcc" in your correspondence according to sound business courtesy and practices. Avoid political motives and emphasize communication in the distribution of letters and memos.

Postscript

In less formal business letters, a postscript may be appropriate. As we pointed out earlier, the P.S. can be used to add emphasis or draw the reader's attention to a critical point. It can also be used to add a personal note to the end of a business letter.

Example: You write a letter to a supplier, requesting a copy of the new catalog. After the signature block, you add a postscript:

> P.S. We hope to see you at the upcoming trade exhibit. Will you have a booth there?

THE FORMAT OF YOUR LETTER

Employees under your supervision should be instructed to use one of
two formats for all letters. The block format, in which every line begins
at the left margin, is the most formal style for business letters by today's
standards. The indented format, involving between five and ten character
spaces at the beginning of each paragraph, is generally considered less
formal.

Both are widely used; both are correct. Which should you use?
Unless your company specifies that a certain format be used company
wide, apply this standard: All letters going outside the organization
should be done in the formal block format, and internal· letters and
memos—which are by their nature less formal—should be prepared in
indented format.

A typical block format letter is shown in Figure 7–1. There is a
double space between paragraphs, and no indentations occur in any part
of the letter. The indented format, shown in Figure 7–2, does not require
extra space between paragraphs. When you use this form, all information
placed to the right should maintain an "internal" left margin.

[*Incorrect*]

Sincerely yours,

Mary C. Smith

MCS:hwd

[*Correct*]

Sincerely yours,

Mary C. Smith

MCS:hwd

Figure 7-1.   Block format.

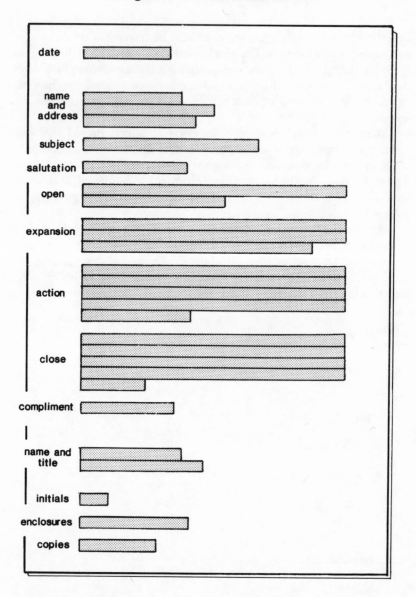

Figure 7-2.   Indented format.

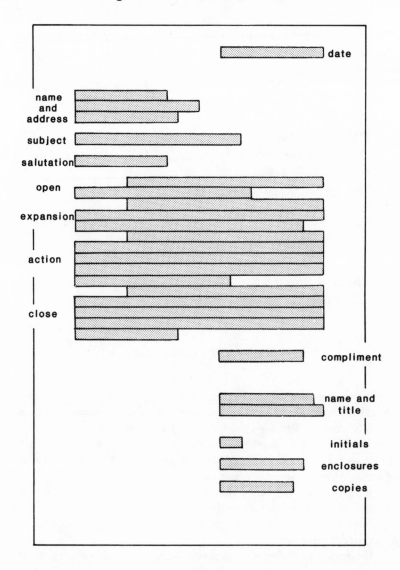

Memos

The memo format is shown in Figure 7-3. When preparing a memo, type the date, to, from, and subject lines with their own internal left margin:

> [*Incorrect*]
>
> DATE: November 12, 1988
> TO: Andrew Brown
> FROM: Terry Smith
> SUBJECT: Annual budget review
>
> [*Correct*]
>
> DATE: November 12, 1988
> TO: Andrew Brown
> FROM: Terry Smith
> SUBJECT: Annual budget review

SPELLING

Spelling is extremely important in written communications. It sends a signal that you are—or are not—educated, intelligent, aware, and careful. Whether you are writing a formal letter to an executive or customer, or a memo to a fellow manager, be sure to check all spelling, including names, before your correspondence goes out. See Appendix B for a list of some words commonly misspelled.

If you use a word processor, you can check your document against the spell checker or dictionary that comes with most programs. If you type letters manually and have a problem with spelling, ask someone else to proofread your work.

If employees under your supervision type letters, a draft should be carefully checked before a final version is typed and sent out. On a word

Figure 7-3.   The memorandum.

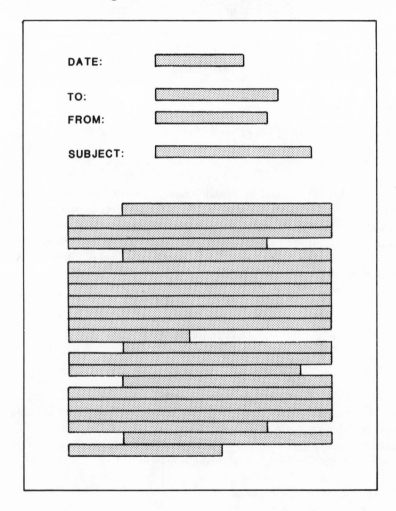

processing system, spelling and appearance should be checked on a draft printout before the final version of the letter is printed.

MARGINS

A letter that is well placed on the page, with appropriate and consistent margins, is pleasing to the eye and easier to read. On a word processing system, consistency of margins is easy. Every correspondence file is set up with instructions for top, bottom, left, and right margins. If your employees type letters, be sure they follow uniform standards.

The date line should be visually associated with the printed information at the top of your letterhead. Skip three spaces between the date and address box. Left, right, and bottom margins should be one inch from the edge of the paper. If your letterhead includes printed information at the bottom of the page, the bottom margin should be calculated from that rather than from the edge.

ENVELOPES

The same basic rules apply to the preparation of envelopes: Pay careful attention to the details of appearance, neatness, and spelling.

The typical business letter is mailed in a standard 9½-inch envelope that includes the company's name and address at the top left. The recipient's name and address should always be typed in the middle of the envelope, aligned on the left, and single-spaced:

Mr. Harold Green, President
HG Enterprises, Inc.
Suite 618
4855 Atlantic Blvd.
Atlantic City, NJ   08404

Notice that the street type is abbreviated. The proper abbreviations are:

Boulevard	Blvd.
Street	St.
Avenue	Ave.
Road	Rd.
Lane	Ln.
Post Office Box	P.O. Box

If you include the room or suite number in the same line as the address, it is also acceptable to abbreviate:

4855 Atlantic Blvd., Ste. 618

The proper abbreviations are:

Suite	Ste.
Room	Rm.
Floor	Fl.

If you write to a department, it is preferable to include that information in the address block. Either format is acceptable, although the second is recommended:

[*Acceptable*]

HG Enterprises, Inc.
Suite 618
4855 Atlantic Blvd.
Atlantic City, NJ   08404
Attn: Accounting Dept.

[*Preferable*]

Accounting Department
HG Enterprises, Inc.
Suite 618
4855 Atlantic Blvd.
Atlantic City, NJ   08404

The rules of correspondence etiquette are basic. Be consistent in applying them and recognize that the overall appearance of your letter makes a lasting impression. The combination of correct spelling, adequate margins, consistency in format, neatness, and the style of communication will convey to the recipient your own level of professionalism.

No one "rule" is absolute when it comes to style or form. We can only make recommendations for sensible and consistent application of standards. For example, your company might establish a policy that all state names are to be spelled out in full. One method can be preferred over another, and that does not make other methods incorrect. To make a professional impression, the rules you adopt should be applied consistently. Develop a standard for drafting letters, document that standard, and expect employees to follow it.

Taking the time and making the effort to perfect your correspondence in every respect affects your own attitude. Once you realize you really *care* about how a document looks when your name is on it, you have made the transition. From that point forward, you are no longer just sending out a letter. You are selling, creating goodwill, and showing a professional attitude in your communications.

WORK PROJECT

1. What is wrong with the following opening to a business letter?

Oct. 10, 1988

Harold Green, Pres.
HG Ent.
4855 Atlantic
Suite 618
Atlantic City, New Jersey 08404

2. You are asked to write a letter to Leslie Brown, whom you have never met. What is the most appropriate salutation?

3. A letter addressed to "Mr. Harold Green, President" closes with the compliment "Best wishes." What change would you make?

8

Improve Your Writing: Uncomplicating the Message

> *"Writing is easy. All you do is stare at a blank sheet of paper until drops of blood form on your forehead."*

> —Gene Fowler

The company had hired a consulting group to conduct a series of internal seminars for middle managers. Each session was designed as a 30-minute lecture on communications skills, but one day the meeting lasted nearly an hour and a half. When one manager arrived back at his desk, an employee asked her what topic had required such a long session.

"Today's subject was the importance of being brief."

Good writing is simple and to the point. That's why you should attempt to limit your letters to one page. This forces you to remove anything that is not absolutely essential.

Another point about good writing: The final result has a sense of ease and simplicity to it, regardless of how difficult it was to arrive there. You might spend many hours writing and rewriting, trying to figure out the strongest opening and the best way to express your thoughts. But the final result simply states, as clearly as possible, what you meant to say. Perhaps the highest compliment you can be paid for your writing is no comment whatsoever—you just get what you ask for.

ACTIVE AND PASSIVE VOICE

Simple, direct communication is more effective than complex, unwieldy sentences. The active voice is more powerful than the passive. In the active voice, the subject of the sentence is the doer of the action described; in the passive voice, the subject is the receiver of the action.

Active   I dropped the ball on that one.

Passive   The ball was dropped by me.

You will get the response you want more often when you use the active voice in your correspondence. Compare the first and second drafts of this assignment letter:

Dear _____:

I would like you to prepare a summary of projects underway in the department. The same format should be used for this summary as the report you did for me last month.

Each project should be listed on the left-hand side of a worksheet, and phases of completion deadlines summarized across. The level of completion should then be filled in, with estimated final dates for subsequent phases indicated.

This summary should be done by the end of this week, time permitting. If that schedule is for any reason impossible, let me know as soon as you can.

I look forward to seeing your work.

Sincerely,

Almost the entire letter is written in the passive voice, which has the effect of weakening your message. Note the difference between these two phrases:

This summary should be done by the end of this week.

You should complete the summary by the end of this week.

The second version is much stronger and more direct than the first. Here's a redrafted version of the complete letter:

[Revised]

Dear _____ :

Please prepare a summary of projects underway in the department. Use the same format as the one in the report you did for me last month.

List each project on the left-hand side of a worksheet, and write in estimated completion deadlines from left to right. Then fill in the level of completion to date, as well as estimated final dates for subsequent phases.

You should complete this summary by the end of this week. If you cannot meet this deadline, please let me know right away.

I look forward to seeing your work.

Sincerely,

When you use the active voice, you vastly improve the tone of your letter. Practice using the active voice to improve your writing skills; see the chart for some examples.

SIMPLIFY THE MESSAGE

You can clarify your writing style by combining the active voice with simple wording. The best letters state their message simply. You should not have to resort to overly complicated phrases when there's a more basic way to say the same thing.

Example: A first draft of a letter explaining a report underway included this paragraph:

Active and Passive Voice

Edit your writing to replace passive voice with active voice whenever possible:

Passive voice	*Active voice*
The report should be done by you and your staff.	You and your staff should do the report.
He was supervised by me.	I supervised him.
The job is being done.	I am doing the job.
That responsibility is mine.	I am responsible.
Your efforts are appreciated.	I appreciate your efforts.
The order will be filled by our shipping department.	Our shipping department will fill the order.
A meeting would be profitable for both of us.	We would both profit from a meeting.

We are currently developing a comprehensive study of the relative historical trends in financial strength, with the variations due to seasonal changes of volume factored in.

Fortunately, this simplified version was substituted before the final memo went out:

[Revised]

We are working on a study of financial trends that includes an allowance for seasonal variation.

Example: A manager wrote a memo to an employee making the following assignment:

Consistent with the analysis you are conducting at this point in time, can you expand your analysis to provide weekly summaries of completion level, cost, and estimated final report? I would like to be kept advised of your progress, as it is essential that I remain cognizant of this project's status.

Here's an alternative that might get a better response:

Please give me a weekly summary of the project you're working on, including level of completion, cost, and your current estimate of final completion date. I want to keep in touch with you while you're working on this project.

In expressing yourself as directly and clearly as possible, avoid the use of unnecessary phrases and business jargon.

Example:

It is imperative that we coordinate the various departments involved in this project, in order that the applicable and appropriate scheduling and timing variables for the current period can be collectively determined.

Or, stated another way:

[Revised]

Department heads should meet to coordinate their schedules for the year, so that this project can be completed on time.

POSITIVE AND NEGATIVE

Write in the active voice, simplify your message, and keep the tone positive. These three things place you far above the average person in terms of writing skills. And these points are not difficult to master; they are just good habits.

Example:

The cognizant management personnel whose participation in the interactive communication sessions concerning estimates of future expenditures are instructed to prepare written documentation for discovered significant incidences of variance.

Or, stated another way:

[Revised]

Managers on the budget committee are to write explanations of all significant variances.

Example:

The issues we discussed are of substantial concern within my area of responsibility. Accordingly, our verbal exchange will neither sufficiently address nor document the indicated responses we might expect from subordinates or one another. Please reduce the essential points you raised to written form and forward your summary to my attention.

Or, stated another way:

[Revised]

You raised several important points when we talked, but I'd like to have them in writing. Please send me a memo listing what you said.

Example:

As a prerequisite, the candidate for this position must be prepared to demonstrate an ability to dispose of the many problematical situations that will confront an individual charged with oversight of multiple procedures and subordinates.

Or, stated another way:

[Revised]

This position requires experience in supervising many people and knowledge of a variety of tasks.

Example:

It is my recommendation that, at our earliest mutual convenience, we should interact during a midday respite. I intend to absorb the cost of this proposed liaison.

Or, stated another way:

[Revised]

Let's have lunch as soon as possible—my treat.

Some types of written communication must convey negative information, but it can still be phrased in a more positive tone. Compare the following phrases:

Negative	*Positive*
Nothing is to leave this department without my prior review and approval.	I must review and approve all work before it's sent out.
The job you did was below your potential, and I now see I will have to supervise you more closely in the future.	I will work more closely with you in future. I know you have the potential for quality.
From the attitude your employee demonstrated on the phone, I can only assume that you are not concerned with customer service.	I am bringing this problem to your attention because I know that you are concerned with customer service.
We could have made our request clearer, but you are still responsible for the error to a greater degree.	Obviously, we each share a portion of the blame. Can we meet to resolve our differences?
It was not appropriate for you to ask for this work directly. In the future, please direct your inquiries to my manager.	Before I provide the work you requested, I must obtain permission from my manager.
Your alternative suggestion is not acceptable. You are to complete the task as I originally directed in my memo to you last week.	I have reviewed your idea and encourage you always to think of alternatives. But in this case, the format cannot be changed.

With a little bit of work, you can make your message positive and even more assertive. There is no need to close channels of communication or to escalate a misunderstanding with harsh and negative words. Maturity and common sense will tell you that diplomacy is always a better alternative. A negative message does not achieve your objective, nor does it enhance the way you are perceived in the organization. Rise above the temptation to strike back or to demand a response, and you will get your way more of the time.

CONSISTENCY OF TONE

In conversation, we alter our tone to reflect statements made by others. We may begin by being friendly, but the other person's hostility quickly makes us defensive. Or, we expect hostility, but the other person's receptivity causes us to adjust to a more friendly tone. That's why a face-to-face meeting is the easiest way to resolve a problem with someone else. A letter, or a series of letters going back and forth, is never as effective as meeting in person to deal with an issue.

When we write, we no longer have the ability to alter our tone in response to the other person. That lack of flexibility is one of the limitations of conveying messages remotely; but in the business world, where the need for documentation is ever-present, correspondence is unavoidable. Therefore, you must use a consistent tone in your letters.

Example: This memo to a vice president asks for approval of a change in procedure:

Dear _____:

The enclosed report proposes a change in our current procedure for processing work orders. I believe this will save time and money, and reduce the need for future staff increases.

Employees in this department are overloaded. We logged more than 80 hours of overtime last month, and something has to be done to correct this problem.

The proposal will not eliminate this problem entirely, but it will

help. The company will further benefit from the efficiency meas-
ures we suggest.

If the proposal is not approved, I anticipate needing to hire an
additional three people within a year, just to keep up. If volume
increases beyond today's level, we will need even more help.

I look forward to your reply.

Sincerely,

Notice that the tone of the letter shifts from the positive discussion of a
proposal for improving procedures to the more negative complaint about
overwork in the department. You can improve this letter with minor
revisions:

[Revised]

Dear _____:

The enclosed report proposes a change in our current
procedure for processing work orders. I believe this will save time
and money and reduce the need for future staff increases.

The trend in overtime in our department supports the
contention in the proposal that a change will reduce costs. I draw
your attention to the statistics on volume of work orders versus
available staff during the past year.

The company will benefit from the proposed new procedures
beyond the immediate relief to this department, as the proposal
shows. Future staff requirements will be significantly reduced
throughout the organization in the coming year as a direct result of
implementing these ideas.

This is not a complete solution, and growth in future volume
will place an additional demand for staffing. But for the immediate
future, I refer you to the analysis of cost savings that are possible
now.

Can we meet next week to discuss this proposal?

Sincerely,

The tone of this second draft is positive and constructive. The same issues are discussed, but from management's point of view more than from the concerns of a department supervisor.

The techniques explained here—active voice, simplicity, positive messages, and consistency of tone—are the tools of good letter writing. Once you master these techniques, you will find that your ability to clarify and express your thoughts will improve.

You will never entirely escape the struggle to develop the best possible method of expressing yourself. No one has ever learned to write easily: Good writing is hard work. But many people go through their lives writing minimally acceptable letters, never quite going from average to excellent. These simple rules can make that difference for you. Practice them and you will notice an immediate change in the tone of your letters and in the way they are preceived by others.

WORK PROJECT

1. Rewrite these passive statements, using the active voice:

   a. The forecast should be completed by us.
   b. A profit was earned by our company this year.
   c. The project was completed on time due to your valuable contribution.

2. Revise this statement to simplify the message:

   The report should be expanded to include the addition of certain applicable visual aids, specifically to summarize financial trends in chart form when appropriate.

3. Turn these negative statements into positive ones:

   a. I received your report, but found it lacking. Come and see me so that I can show you how to improve it.
   b. Don't send the statement out until I've had the chance to check your math.
   c. It's obvious from your request that you have no appreciation of the deadlines we're under.

9

Listen to Your Words: The Rhythm of Your Letter

"It's not a bad idea to get in the habit of writing down one's thoughts. It saves one having to bother anyone else with them."

—Isabel Colegate

"I received another memo from the vice president," Beth told Frank. "I swear, he writes like Shakespeare."

"Do you mean that he's a good writer?"

"No. I mean that each line has ten syllables and no one understands what he's saying without a synopsis!"

Writing simply is an admirable skill. A simple, well-written letter clearly states what you mean. It also has a rhythm of its own. The reader's ability to perceive your message is affected by not only how clearly you communicate but also by your writing style.

SENTENCE LENGTH

Be aware of the reader's "ear." A monotonous rhythm will put the reader to sleep, regardless of the message and its clarity.

Example: In a memo to an employee, a manager includes this paragraph:

> The report should be as accurate as possible. Avoid estimates or vague references. Research your facts thoroughly. Go to other departments to gather information. And see me if you run into problems.

As you read this, are you aware of the sing-song tone of the sentences? They're all about the same length and meter (number of syllables), which makes for tiring reading. A revised version could read:

> *[Revised]*
>
> The report should be as accurate as possible, without estimates or vague references. Research your facts thoroughly. Go to other departments to gather information and see me if you run into problems.

In this version, five sentences have been reduced to three. The sentence in the middle, which is a very important point, is emphasized by its shortness. As a result, this version is much easier to read.

Combining short, choppy sentences into more coherent thoughts is only one way of improving a sentence's rhythm. The important point is to vary length and meter. You can use this technique to add emphasis and keep the reader's interest. The same message could be made more dramatic by writing it like this:

> Strive for accuracy in the report. We want facts, not estimates of vague estimates. Research. That's what it's going to take. Go to other departments to gather information and see me if you run into problems.

A solitary word is not a legitimate sentence if you strictly follow the rules of grammar. But in your communications, you need emphasis, clarity, and variety to get and hold the reader's attention. If you must highlight something—say, the need for research—this is a very effective way to do it.

PARAGRAPHS

The same rules of variety apply to paragraphs. Just as you can emphasize an important point with a short sentence, a key issue can be highlighted with a one-sentence paragraph.

In business writing, where narrative and outline forms are often combined, the rules for dividing units of thought into paragraph form are more relaxed than in many other written forms. But you must still be aware of the need to control and vary the length of your thoughts.

Example: One manager is in the habit of writing memos in a regimented format. His memos and letters all look about the same; every paragraph is three to four sentences long. In terms of appearance alone, they are difficult to read.

Here's the first draft of a letter he wrote responding to a customer complaint:

Dear _____:

Thank you for your letter of November 2. I am sorry to hear that you were unsatisfied with your shipment, and I appreciate your taking the time to write.

I have contracted the sales office that sent your shipment to you and asked them to deliver a replacement at once. In addition, I have asked the manager to review quality procedures.

I can assure you that we are very concerned with maintaining the goodwill of our valued customers. This oversight was an unfortunate exception.

If, for any reason, you are not pleased with the replacement you

receive, let me know at once. Again, thank you for bringing this to
my attention.

Sincerely,

Notice that each paragraph is about the same length. While the tone of
communication is direct and does address the issue, some variety would
help emphasize some parts of the letter.

[Edited]

Dear _____:

Thank you for your letter of November 2. I appreciate your taking
the time to write.

I am sorry to hear that you were unsatisfied with your shipment
and I have contacted the sales office that sent it to you. They will
deliver a replacement at once. In addition, I have asked the
manager to review quality procedures.

I can assure you that we are very concerned with maintaining the
goodwill of our valued customers. This oversight was an unfortunate exception. If, for any reason, you are not pleased with the
replacement you receive, just let me know.

Again, thank you for bringing this to my attention.

Sincerely,

Here the units of thought are divided up so that the beginning and
ending are given more significance. In this case, the middle parts provide
details, and the primary message is, "We care about our customers, and
thank you for letting us know there is a problem."

THE KEY WORD IN EACH SENTENCE

With a little practice you can easily learn to fit rhythm and variety into your letters. The best way to develop this skill is to write a first draft and then go through again, checking your letter with a reader's ear. It helps to read aloud. With that technique, you will quickly pick up on redundancies of tone. After practicing for a while, you will discover that the "reader's ear" sensitivity becomes second nature.

You must be concerned, of course, with continuity. A letter or memo must flow with a strength of focus, as well as with ease and style. Combine clarity with a conversational tone, and you create a message that will be read and understood by others.

To ensure continuity, go over your first draft and identify the key word or words in each sentence. That word should be related to your focus and should advance the message you want to send. In the response letter to the customer, for example, the key words are:

Letter	*Key Words*
Thank you for your letter of November 2. I appreciate your taking the time to write.	Thank you I appreciate
I am sorry to hear that you were unsatisfied with your shipment and I have contacted the sales office that sent it to you. They will deliver a replacement at once. In addition, I have asked the manager to review quality procedures.	I am sorry replacement quality
I can assure you that we are very concerned with maintaining the goodwill of our valued customers. This oversight was an unfortunate exception. If, for any reason, you are not pleased with the replacement you receive, just let me know.	we are concerned oversight If you are not pleased let me know
Again, thank you for bringing this to my attention.	thank you

Notice that the string of key words identifies the focus of the message this letter intends to convey. If an unneeded paragraph were included, it would become apparent at once that the focus was wandering.

This technique can also be used in the preparation of a draft. Before writing your letter, outline the key points you intend to communicate and in the order you want to state them. Then, with that clarity of focus, you will be able to draft a brief but strong message.

FINDING YOUR OWN STYLE

People who communicate effectively get results. And results help you advance in your career. Find your own personal style of communicating in writing, and set standards for yourself.

Recognize these facts about communications within your organization:

1. Simple, clear messages get results.
2. Expressing priorities and asking for action are what business is all about.
3. While written correspondence is necessary to create documentation, it is not as effective as a personal meeting and discussion.
4. Successful careers are built on good communication skills.

How can writing an effective letter or memo advance your career? First, if you believe that delegation is a mark of a good manager, you must learn to make assignments and see them through. If you can write an effective assignment memo, you will improve your delegation skills.

An educated person might have the vocabulary to draft long memos that no one else can read. But an experienced person develops the insight to draft short memos that no one else can write. This is the key. Don't fall into the trap of believing that long documents are more important; they're not. In fact, they're more likely to be glossed over by the recipient, creating the exact opposite effect.

Respect the value of time in your organization. Few people can afford the luxury of reading a large number of proposals, reports, and memos; in larger organizations, there's an endless stream of messages. If you want to make a difference and have an impact on the company, write briefly and clearly. A memo of two sentences that gets a response is much better than one of two pages that gets filed—unread.

The ability to communicate well and consistently is rare. That's unfortunate but true. If you want your career to be successful, concentrate your efforts in both oral and written communication skills. Others in the company—subordinates, other managers, and executives—will identify you as a clear communicator. You will then gain the reputation of being dependable. If you communicate well, you become well defined.

Think of the managers and executives you know. Some are unpredictable. You never know what motivates them or how they will react to something you suggest. They might not come through with their promises, or they might be inconsistent in their responses. Working with someone like that is far from enjoyable.

Now consider the other managers or executives you know. They're always in control, they express themselves well, and you always know where you stand with them. They confront problems in an adult, healthy manner. Instead of making enemies and alienating people, they concentrate on achieving goals and executing assignments. Their subordinates are happier because they know where they stand and what's expected of them.

Next, compare these vastly different personalities from the perspective of top management. If you were president of the company, which would you be mostly likely to promote in the future? Just as you enjoy working with someone you understand and can depend on, so does top management. And that means people who communicate well. These people can delegate to employees within a department, they operate with clear and well-expressed goals, and they come through when others depend on performance.

Communication is the real key to success here. If you are able to identify and explain problems, propose positive solutions, and demonstrate results, you are already a success. Sadly, a lot of people spend their careers struggling with communication skills and never quite grasping the simple truth. Don't fall into that trap.

Be sensitive to others, structure your written communications from the reader's point of view, and anticipate the range of possible responses. Look for unintentional tones in your letters that might alienate someone, and remove those tones. Combine diplomacy with good intentions and common sense, and your communications will be well received. Recognize and respect the fact that not everyone sees one issue in the same way. Cultural differences, perspectives from an isolated division or department, and personalities all contribute to the inherent problem of communicating.

None of those problems is easily solved. It takes hard work, sensitivity, and sometimes many hours to resolve problems. A short memo may take much more time to write than a long one, but the results are worth your efforts. Proceed with the attitude that communicating clearly and effectively is actually an investment in your own future.

WORK PROJECT

1. Revise this paragraph to improve its rhythm:

> We provide this service to approximately 35 companies in the state. We can demonstrate to you that you can save money with the right plan. And we emphasize that objective when we put a program together. We'd like to show you how our program works.

2. List the key words in your revised draft of the paragraph above. Look for clarity of focus.

3. Write a different version of the paragraph that expresses the principal message more clearly.

Appendix A
Work Project Answers

1. It's important to develop a sense of how your statements will be received. Softening the tone of a statement produces good communications. For example:

    a. Please respond by Friday at the latest, or let me know well in advance if this deadline is a problem.
    b. To proceed, we need to hear from you as quickly as possible. Please call me when you receive this letter.
    c. I know our deadlines often create a strain on your resources. I'd appreciate a call from you if you won't be able to get back to us on time.

2. Openings are important because they set the tone of the entire letter. You can easily lose the reader before you even get started, unless you take the time to set a friendly tone:

    a. I know I seem to be constantly asking for a quick response at the last minute, and I hope you understand that we are also given a short deadline.
    b. I think we can resolve this problem with a face-to-face meeting. Let's get together right away.
    c. Thanks so much for coming through when we really needed your help.

3. Remember that strong closing statements wrap up the letter and

create a response, and weak ones trail off and set the mood for nonresponse. Make your endings as strong and supportive as possible:

    a. Can you make a Wednesday deadline?
    b. Let me know if I can do anything to help out with this project.
    c. I hope this was an isolated incident. Can we depend on you in the
       future?

CHAPTER 2

1. This letter is aggressive and will offend the reader, perhaps preventing any positive response. A more tactful version:

Dear _____:

    This is a follow-up to our previous request for a status report.
    We are up against a deadline at the end of this week, and would appreciate a fast response, your schedule permitting. Can you let me know when we should expect the report?

        Sincerely,

2. When making a request to someone in the company who outranks you, be especially careful. Phrase your letter so that it won't offend. For example:

Dear _____:

    We are working on our monthly executive committee report, which includes your own summary.
    Please let us know if there will be a delay this month so that we can advise committee members.

        Sincerely,

3. An outright refusal will only create bad feelings. A more diplomatic approach is to forward the letter to your supervisor along with a copy of your response, which should read something like this:

Dear _____:

    I received your request for a departmental report. However, my supervisor has always handled budgetary reports in the past, and I hesitate to respond directly to your request.
    I have forwarded your letter to my supervisor. If she instructs me to respond, I will be glad to assist you in any way possible.

Sincerely,

CHAPTER 3

1. The problem with the statements is that they are overly assertive. You need to emphasize the importance of your request, but be aware of the danger in stating your demands too strongly. Some alternatives:

    a. I would appreciate an immediate response, if your schedule permits. Please let me know if this request creates a conflict for you.
    b. Our deadline for completion is one month. I'd appreciate a full report by March 1.
    c. Please give me a call as soon as you've had the chance to review this letter.

2. Look for excessive words and phrases and eliminate whatever is not needed:

    a. detailed analysis
       complete analysis
       analysis ("detailed" or "complete" might already be understood)
    b. as you know
       you must know that
    c. this year
    d. in the future

3. The example is weak, as it hedges the request and does not ask for a response by the deadline. An alternative:

> **We have scheduled.completion of this project for the end of the month. Please let me know if this creates a conflict for you.**

CHAPTER 4

1. A complete promotional campaign contains more than letters— even good ones. The letter, while important, is not the entire story. You might suggest expanding the procedure to include:

A followup phone call
A second latter, regardless of response
A final attempt
Acknowledgment of appointments
A followup letter several months later

2. You should respond as quickly as possible to all customer complaint letters. Be sure you make it clear that you do listen to what they have to say and that your response is more than a form letter. Promise immediate action and make sure you carry through on your promise. Also consider getting in touch with the customer later, to make sure he or she is now satisfied. The tone of your letter can make a big difference in keeping customers happy.

3. An assignment letter must be as concise as possible. It should include:

a.   An exact description of what you want done
b.   A response deadline
c.   A request for a response if there's a problem
d.   An invitation for alterntive ideas

CHAPTER 5

1. Keep in mind that your opening paragraph will set the tone for your entire letter. When responding to a customer complaint, take a very direct approach. For example:

I appreciated your taking the time to write and bring to my attention the problem you experienced with our branch office. I can assure you that we want to resolve this to your complete satisfaction.

2. Your action should relate specifically to the problem the customer experienced. If appropriate, promise to see to it personally that the problem will be resolved at once. Actions could include:

a. Calling a field office and insisting on immediate corrective action
b. An evaluation of supervisory procedures, perhaps adding control points to avoid a repeat
c. Follow-up with the customer at a later date

3. A closing question should cause the reader to want to respond. For example:

a. Can we meet in your office on Tuesday?
b. Would you like to hear more?
c. Can we visit with you this week?

CHAPTER 6

1. Unfortunately, any effort at communicating has the potential to lead to problems. But if you are aware of the special problems you might face in business communications, you improve your chances of success. Here are possible interpretations of requests you make. Be aware of them and draft your letters to eliminate the problem:

a. From the president of the company:

"Who are you, to give assignments to me?"
"I'm far too busy to give you the time you're asking for."
"Ask my secretary to help you."

b. From a fellow department manager:

"Why are you prying into my department? It's none of your
business."

"Why can't you find this information on your own?"

"Are you planning to take credit for my efforts?"

c. From an employee:

"You're always telling me what to do, but I never get any
recognition for my hard work."

"You give a lot of assignments, but I don't always understand
what you really want."

"I'm far too busy with other work you've already given me
to do this job, too."

2. Don't let the misunderstanding continue or get worse. Confront
the issues directly, preferably in person. If there's too much anger to
communicate that way, write a letter apologizing for the misunderstanding. Identify with the other person's point of view and explain exactly
what you need and want. The next time you write, take the time to
phrase your request more diplomatically.

3. A good transition clarifies your message and makes it easier for
the recipient to respond. With a little thought, you can draft a transition
from one request to another. For example, you end your first request
paragraph with:

. . . and I've taken the liberty of including a worksheet for the format
in which I need the historical summary.

Now, to also request a preliminary forecast, you might try:

This worksheet serves two purposes. In addition to the historical
information, the coming year's income forecast follows the same
format.

In addition to the historical summary, can you also provide a brief
preliminary forecast of next year's income?

My request has a second part. I will also need . . .

CHAPTER 7

1. Several features in this opening need to be corrected.

   a. The date should not be abbreviated. It should read:

      October 10, 1988

   b. The name should be spelled out in full, including the complete title:

      Mr. Harold Green, President

   c. The company name should not be abbreviated; spell out the complete name:

      HG Enterprises

   d. The suite number should be placed on a line before the street address, or included on the same line.

   e. A preferred style is to include no commas and to abbreviate the state:

      Atlantic City NJ   08404

2. Because you do not know the person, it is appropriate to address by title: "Mr." or "Ms." But the name "Leslie" could belong to either sex. In this case, the best alternative is to write your salutation as:

   Dear Leslie Brown:

3. Do not mix formal salutations with informal compliments. Replace "Best wishes" with something more formal, such as "Sincerely yours." Or, if you intend the informal, change the salutation to a first-name basis and leave the compliment in its less formal style.

CHAPTER 8

1. Identify the subject of the sentences, then revise them so that the subject acts rather than receives the action:

    a. We should complete the forecast.
    b. Our company earned a profit this year.
    c. Your valuable contribution enabled us to complete the project on time.

2. Do away with the unneeded words and you can state this message very simply:

    To add clarity, our report should include charts that reveal financial information.

3. Avoid sending negative messages through poorly conceived ideas. Virtually anything you have to say can be expressed in a positive tone:

    a. Thank you for the report you submitted. Please see me so that we can discuss adding more detail to it.
    b. Let's ensure absolute accuracy in all work we send out. Send statements to me for a second review.
    c. Your request points out the need for better communication between our departments. I'd like to meet with you this week to help resolve this problem.

CHAPTER 9

1. Once you have stated your message clearly, read it over, looking for monotonous rhythm. It's easily fixed, just by varying sentence length. For example:

    We provide this service to approximately 35 companies in the state and we can demonstrate that you can save money with the right plan. We emphasize that objective. May we show you how our program works?

2. The key words identify and reaffirm your focus. In this case, those key words are:

> We provide . . . service . . . can demonstrate . . . you can save money . . . emphasize . . . objective . . . May we show you . . .

3. You can rewrite a paragraph to shift emphasis and remove unnecessary words. But in the process, be sure not to sacrifice rhythm and focus. In a sales letter, you can add drama to your letters with selective use of the one-word sentence. For example:

> You can save money with the right plan, as our 35 local customers already know. That's what we emphasize. Results. Give us a chance to show you how our program works.

Appendix B:

Punctuation and Usage Quick-Check

INTRODUCTION

The following section presents recommendations and guidelines for many of the common problems you will encounter in punctuation and usage. If you supervise a diverse staff of employees, one of the problems you face is establishing a logical and consistent set of rules. This is because:

1. English is less than precise.
2. Employees have different cultural and educational backgrounds.
3. Companies' rules and practices vary.
4. Employees are inconsistent in following rules of usage.
5. Standards for business letters continually change.

Some organizations develop their own style and usage guidelines, although in many cases the question of consistency is not addressed formally. Rules are devised in departments without uniform guidelines or written policies. If your company doesn't have written standards, it is up to you to develop guidelines on your own. The following recommendations will help you in training your staff, establishing standards, and enforcing them.

The Appendix includes these sections:

Punctuation hints: the forms of punctuation and their proper usage.

Good usage guidelines: recommendations for setting standards for abbreviations, capitalization, numbers, percents, and underlining.

Commonly misused words: words that are frequently misused and their proper definitions.

Commonly misspelled words: words that have spelling variations or are frequently misspelled.

Useful references: books that offer you additional help.

You will not be able to identify the "right" way to express a thought in every case. Form and usage guidelines should be thought of as recommendations only, to be used to set standards for consistency. If your organization does not publish its own guidelines, recommend that a written policy be established to handle questions of style and usage.

PUNCTUATION HINTS

apostrophe Use in contracted words *(don't, doesn't)* and in possessives *(John's report, the company's standard, workers' rights)*.

asterisk Used to footnote or annotate a reference that (1) does not fit in the thought or (2) is a secondary idea.

The loss for the year* also reduced the market's perception of future growth potential.

*The loss was due to a one-time extraordinary adjustment.

bar Also called the slant or slash, the bar is used in place of a conjunction *(and, or)*.

the April/May/June quarter

brackets Indicates material added in a quotation that is not part of the quote.

He went along with [the proposal].

colon   Use with a short list, a salutation, or time of day.

> We use two versions: current and year-to-date.
>
> Dear Mr. Smith:
>
> 3:30 p.m.

comma   Offsets a second thought in a sentence, interrupts a primary thought, distinguishes two unrelated ideas in one sentence, separates a series of words or phrases, or divides adjectives. Also used within numbers, dates, city and state names, to precede a short quotation, and to add clarity between two unrelated numbers.

> The department, newly formed last year, reports to the vice president.
>
> The report, though, was not correct.
>
> He plans to attend the meeting, which promises to be a productive one.
>
> Offices are located in New York, San Francisco, Chicago, St. Louis, and Los Angeles.
>
> It was a clear, focused letter.
>
> We earned $18,456,000 last year.
>
> December 15, 1988
>
> Atlanta, Georgia
>
> He answered, "Yes, by Monday."
>
> During 1988, 14 employees were hired.

dash   Offsets a separate thought. (On a typewriter, use double hyphen.)

> Letters—other than those written in response to an extended list of questions—should be limited to one page.
>
> The manager—normally a capable employee—made significant errors in the report.

ellipsis Used to indicate deletions in a quotation, a pause, or an incomplete thought. When the ellipsis occurs within the sentence, use three periods; at the end of the sentence, use four (one for the period and three for the ellipsis).

> "They . . . met with the board."

> The decision was delayed . . . and then delayed again.

> If only we'd met beforehand. . . .

exclamation mark Ends a sentence with emphasis. Usage in business letters should be rare.

> They reversed their position again!

> Now they say we never wrote to them!

hyphen Used to connect related words:

> year-to-date

> go-between

> ready-made

> short- and long-term

parenthesis Used as an alternative to commas or dashes to separate an unrelated thought within a sentence, to expand on a preceding statement, to refer to a source, for abbreviations after a full name or title, or to offset elements of an outline or a list.

> The report (on production) was sent to every manager.

> Mr. Adams (vice president of operations) was in attendance.

> Production declined by 14% (figures supplied by the marketing department).

> Internal Revenue Service (IRS)

> (a) sick days

(b) vacation
(c) holidays

period   Marks the end of a sentence or abbreviation. Examples of use in abbreviations:

et cetera	etc.
Incorporated	Inc.
February	Feb.
Mister	Mr.
Monday	Mon.

question mark   Signifies the end of an interrogatory statement. As a general rule, don't use more than one, although occasional use for emphasis is acceptable:

What does this mean??

quotation marks   Used for direct quotes or to indicate slang or jargon. For a quote within a quote, use single quotation marks.

He said, "The check was mailed to you this morning."

He insisted on "data integrity" in the report.

He argued, "I heard them say 'Stop' so I waited."

semicolon   Used to distinguish multiple thoughts within one sentence.

The report contained a summary; supplements from divisions four, seven, and nine; and recommendations.

GOOD USAGE GUIDELINES

abbreviations   Should be used in a complete sentence only when part of a name or title.

[Correct]

Mr. Smith is president of the company.

[Incorrect]

Mr. Smith is pres. of the co.

Follow shortened words with a period, but avoid periods within abbreviations. For example, "IRS" is preferred over "I.R.S."

capitalization The first word of every sentence is to be capitalized (including a complete thought following a colon), as are all proper nouns and abbreviations of organizations.

This is the report we promised.

This belongs to the Boston branch office.

We sent the return to the IRS.

It was simple: He didn't complete the job.

Capitalization can also be used to emphasize a key word or phrase, although be careful of overuse.

numbers Write out the number if under 10, abbreviate if 10 or more. When a single sentence contains mixed usage, express all in figures.

We have five months until the deadline.

Include all 12 months in the report.

Only 5 of the 12 months show a variance.

Regardless of the first rules, numbers appearing at the beginning of a sentence should *always* be spelled out:

Thirty-five employees have been hired.

Avoid mixing numerical systems.

[Wrong]

The IV Section reported 11 new jobs.

[Right]

Section Four reported 11 new jobs.

Do not use ordinal numbers ("1st," "2nd") in the text of a letter.

[Wrong]

We reported a 2nd quarter profit.

[Right]

We reported a second-quarter profit.

Ordinals are acceptable in street addresses and sometimes in tabular material.

percent   We recommend spelling out "percent" when used without a corresponding number; use the symbol when part of a number (14%).

underlining   Used to indicate emphasis as with italics, in reference sections of letters, or to highlight sections of an outline.

We <u>must</u> meet the deadline.

Subject: <u>Smith vs. Hanson Corp.</u>

Section III: <u>Market Analysis</u>

COMMONLY MISUSED WORDS

accept   to receive
except   to exclude

advice   an opinion
advise   to offer an opinion or information

affect   to influence
effect   to create or cause; a result

allude   to imply or state indirectly
elude   to avoid or escape

allusion   a reference to another subject
illusion   a false belief or appearance

already   by now
all ready   everyone or everything is ready

altogether   completely
all together   everyone or everything

among   with three or more
between   with two

ascent   rise
assent   permission

beside   next to
besides   in addition to

biannual   twice a year
biennial   every two years

can   is able
may   has permission

complement   a piece that provides completion
compliment   praise

conscious   aware of
conscience   awareness of right and wrong

continual   in succession
continuous   without stop

council   a committee or group
counsel   to give suggestions or advice; an attorney

credible   likely or believable
creditable   admirable or deserving

definite   absolute
definitive   conclusive or exact

detract   to take away
distract   to harass or preoccupy

discreet   prudent
discrete   separate

each other   two
one another   more than two

eminent   noteworthy
imminent   impending

extant   intact, preserved
extent   degree

farther   reference to measurable distance
further   in addition to

forego   go before
forgo   go without

in   within
into   in reference to entering

incredible   not to be believed
incredulous   skeptical

ingenious   skilled, able
ingenuous   candid

interstate   between different states
intrastate   within one state

last   the final
latest   the most recent

later   after
latter   the second of two things

lay   to put down
lie   to recline

may be   a verb implying possibility
maybe   an adverb meaning perhaps

persecute   to chase or harass
prosecute   to bring legal action

practical   of use
practicable   possible

precede   to come before
proceed   to go forward

principal   of higher rank
principle   truth or idea

respectful   with respect
respective   in regard to

set   to place
sit   to assume a sitting position

stationary   unmoving
stationery   supplies for the office

COMMONLY MISSPELLED WORDS

English spelling, like punctuation and usage, is not subject to consistent or constant rules. Many words have spelling variations, and not every dictionary is in agreement on what is correct. The following list contains the recommended spelling for words that have variations and the correct spelling for words that are commonly misspelled.

absence	accessible	accommodate
achievement	acknowledgment	acquire
addenda	advantageous	adviser
advisory	affect	affidavit
aggrieved	all right	analogous
analysis	analyze	anomaly
apparent	argument	auxiliary
belief	believe	beneficial
benefited	bona fide	by-product
calendar	caliber	cancelled
cancellation	catalog	category
coming	commitment	comparative

concede	conscious	consensus
controversy	controversial	cooperate
coordinate	copyright	corollary
correctable	correlation	counselor
crystallize	curriculums	defense
definitely	definition	describe
description	device	diagrammed
diagrammatic	dilapidated	disastrous
discernible	disk	echelon
effect	eligible	embarrass
eminent	employee	enclose
encyclopedia	entrust	environment
exaggerate	excellence	excerpt
existent	experience	explanation
facetious	farfetched	fascinate
feasibility	fictitious	focused
forcibly	foreword	formulas
fulfill	gamut	gauge
glamorous	glamour	glossary
grievance	harass	height
hierarchical	hierarchy	hodgepodge
idiosyncrasy	imminence	impatient
indefatigable	independent	indispensable
inert	inquiry	inspector
intellect	interest	jeopardize
judgment	judiciary	juncture
juvenile	juxtapose	keypunch
knowledgeable	led	leveling
liaison	licensee	licensor
likable	linear	losing
maintenance	manageable	mandatory
maneuver	marriage	marshaled
measurable	medieval	mileage
misspell	naive	necessary
necessitate	negligent	negligible
nonplussed	noticeable	notwithstanding
nucleus	obsession	obsolescence
obsolete	occasion	occur

occurred	occurrence	occurring
offbeat	offhanded	oftentimes
opinion	opportunity	paid
paralyze	particular	penetrate
perceptible	performance	permanent
personal	personnel	persuasive
phraseology	possible	practical
practice	precede	predicate
predominant	preempt	preexisting
prejudice	preoccupy	prepare
prerequisite	presumptuous	prevalent
principal	principle	privilege
probably	procedure	proceed
processor	profession	professor
programmed	prominent	prototype
publicly	pursue	purveyor
quantitative	questionnaire	queuing
quiescent	quiet	quit
quite	quorum	quota
rapport	rarefied	receive
recommend	reconcile	reconnoiter
recur	recurrence	reestablish
reexamine	referring	repetition
rhythm	sacrilegious	salable
semiannual	sense	separate
separation	serviceable	shining
similar	sizable	skeptic
stabilize	straitjacket	studying
subcommittee	succeed	succession
supersede	surprise	synonymous
technique	than	their
then	there	they're
thorough	threshold	to
too	trail	trial
transferred	traveler	tremendous
uncorroborated	unduly	unnecessary
unprincipled	validate	vendor
vice versa	viewpoint	villian

wholly	willpower	workday
work flow	work force	workload
worthwhile	wrongdoing	wrongful

USEFUL REFERENCES

The Elements of Style, W. Strunk, Jr., and E. B. White (New York: Macmillan Publishing Co., 1979).

Webster's Ninth New Collegiate Dictionary (Springfield, Mass.: G. & C. Merriam Company, 1987).

The Chicago Manual of Style, 13th edition (Chicago: The University of Chicago Press, 1982).

Words into Type, third edition, (Englewood Cliffs, N.J.: Prentice-Hall, Inc., 1974).

A Dictionary of Modern English Usage, second edition. H. W. Fowler (New York: Oxford University Press, 1965).

Roget's International Thesaurus, fourth edition (New York: Harper & Row, 1977).

Index